CW01656117

Assault at Mogadishu

Assault at Mogadishu

by

Peter Koch and Kai Hermann

Translated and Edited by John Man

CORGI BOOKS
A DIVISION OF TRANSWORLD PUBLISHERS LTD

ASSAULT AT MOGADISHU

A CORGI BOOK 0 552 10774 3

First publication in Great Britain

PRINTING HISTORY
Corgi edition published 1977

Corgi Books are published by Transworld Publishers Ltd,
Century House, 61–63 Uxbridge Road,
Ealing, London, W.5.
Filmset by Keyspools Ltd, Golborne, Lancashire.
Printed in Great Britain by
Cox & Wyman Ltd, London, Reading and Fakenham.

CONTENTS

ACKNOWLEDGEMENTS

The core of this book was devised by Peter Koch and Kai Herrmann of STERN. It was revised for an English readership. The first two chapters represent additional material. Thanks are due to Elspeth Purchase and Fleur Walsh without whom the book could not have been completed on time.

J.M.

1. CONNECTIONS

It was like another Entebbe.

For five days, from October 13–18, two men and two women held hostage the passengers and crew of a Lufthansa 737 from Majorca. No one knew who the hijackers were. Led by a wildly unstable sadist who identified himself only as 'Captain Mahmud', the four demanded the release from West Germany of eleven convicted terrorists. Seeking haven, Mahmud ordered the plane to Cyprus, to Dubai, to Aden (where Mahmud, suspecting the plane's captain of trying to escape, screamed at him: 'Are you guilty? Are you guilty?' and shot him in the head), and finally to Mogadishu in Somalia, on the Horn of Africa.

There, on the night of October 17–18, the plane sat in the steamy tropical darkness. The Germans had until 2.30 a.m., Mahmud had said, to deliver the prisoners, otherwise the plane and its 86 hostages would be blown up.

The Germans never had any intention of giving in. Five years before, a bungled attempt to rescue nine Israeli hostages taken by Palestinians during the Munich Olympics had led to a massacre. Since then, a special commando group had been in training for just such an occasion as this. That night, the commandos' plane landed at Mogadishu, on a far runway, its lights out.

Twenty-eight commandos crept stealthily under the rear of the hijacked plane. At 1.50 a.m. Somali soldiers created a diversion by lighting a fire on the runway. The terrorists gathered in the cockpit. At 2.07 a.m. commandos leapt on the wings, blew in the emergency doors and tossed in special 'stun' grenades which temporarily blinded and deafened the occupants. After a few seconds, the Germans burst in. Three of the terrorists were shot dead; the fourth, a woman, took refuge in a lavatory and fired wildly through the door. The fire was returned and she was severely wounded. But the passengers were safe.

The news sent a wave of delight and exhilaration around the world. Thc *Daily Mail* headlined the brilliant rescue by 'the Desert Foxes'. New York's *Daily News* offered West Germany 'the praise and admiration of the civilized world'. The German Embassy in Washington was beseiged with calls of congratulations. In Japan, Africa, Europe – across the whole world – radio and television stations praised the 'heroes of Mogadishu'.

The raid was not, in fact, exactly comparable to Entebbe. In June, 1976, when Israelis rescued the hostages of the Air France flight hijacked to Uganda by Palestinians, they had mounted a miniature military invasion on hostile territory; about 50 people had died. At Mogadishu, the Germans had the co-operation of the local forces. There was no battle. The only dead were the three terrorists. There was no need for a rapid getaway. But it was meticulously planned and dramatically efficient – a brilliant end to a piece of senseless terrorism.

It is also part of a wider story, of the peculiarly vicious form of terrorism that has emerged internationally in the 1970's. In particular, it is a story that concerns West Germany, where those who follow Andreas Baader and Ulrike Meinhof have established the most long-lasting terrorist cell in the western world.

The Baader-Meinhof group represents an extraordinary phenomenon: pure destructiveness for its own sake. They are not terrorists with genuine left-wing sympathies – they do not wish to overthrow a particular regime and replace it with another (as, for instance, the guerrillas of a number of South American countries, do); nor do they seek a separatist identity (as the Basque terrorists do); nor do they operate for pure cash, like those who kidnapped the Dutch millionaire

Maurits Caransa in November 1977. They seek only to destroy the society that shelters them. Though their origins lie in the political Left, they do not any longer aim to help any particular section of society. They are anti-idealists. Some of them advocate violence for its own sake. Although they have links with other terrorist groups, in particular the Palestinians, they seldom even try to disguise their actions with the veneer of left-wing political vocabulary.

In September, 1977, after a number of killings and kidnappings, the Baader-Meinhof gang abducted Hanns Martin Schleyer, one of the country's top business men. West Germany reacted as if to an armed assault. The country became an armed camp. Government buildings were sandbagged and protected with barbed-wire. All ministers were given bodyguards; businesses clamoured for bullet-proof cars. At the borders, young guards with sub-machine guns slung over their shoulders stopped and searched thousands of cars. Houses and flats were searched by the thousand, road blocks were set up, identification checks became routine.

Many of these measures violated the spirit and in many cases the letter of West Germany's carefully worked out Constitution, which sought to guarantee the freedom of the individual against any encroaching authority on the part of the state. Now, with scarcely a murmur, that freedom was being undermined.

All this marked the beginning of what proved to be an extraordinary sequence of interlocking events. The German government's tough line on terrorism led to the second terrorist response – the hijacking of the Lufthansa jet by Palestinians who, with a surrealistically topsy-turvy view of history, saw an 'imperialist' alliance between the 'Nazi' German state of today and 'Zionism'. Germany's determination not to give in ended in the early morning of October 18 on the tarmac at Mogadishu. But this in its turn led to yet another startling development: the suicide of three Baader-Meinhof leaders in their top-security cells in Stammheim Prison (a fourth suicide occurred in mid-November).

This story is all of a piece: it hangs togther like a well

constructed thriller. But it is also part of a continuing battle with terrorism. On November 9, shortly before this book went to press, the West German magazine *Stern* reported that Iraqi-trained West German terrorists had returned to Europe to revenge the failure of the kidnapping of Schleyer and the Lufthansa hijacking.

Many people in West Germany talk as if they were engaged in a civil war. It seems at first like an exaggeration; what, after all, can a dozen terrorists achieve against a state? But, as Schleyer's killing showed, a few terrorists can convince a whole nation that it is on the brink of war and force its leaders to deal with them as equals. Indeed, the most effective response – as the assault at Mogadishu showed – is that of a nation at war.

The terrorists were, if not successful, at least effective. They struck at the roots of their society, and may permanently have changed it. So far the problem has been a predominantly German one. But all western societies are similarly vulnerable. There is a pattern in these events which with little variation could fit any western nation. Tomorrow, next year, it could happen here.

2. ORIGINS

The group known as Baader-Meinhof was formed in May 1970, but its origins go back to the student unrest of the mid-1960's, a phenomenon which spread across Europe and America and involved many sections of society in varying degrees of protest.

The focus of the protest movement was the Vietnam War, but there were many other issues at stake. In West Germany there was particular opposition to German rearmament and the building of the Berlin Wall. Most of the groups formed at this time shared a more or less Marxist view of society, but there were widespread differences over the means to be used to effect social change. The vast majority of students and radical sympathizers favoured peaceful methods – demonstrations, sit-ins, strikes. But such methods proved inadequate and many protesters began to advocate open defiance of the law.

In April 1967 there were huge demonstrations in West Berlin to protest to the visiting United States Vice-President, Hubert Humphrey, the growing war in Vietnam. Students clashed with police and the offices of the newly formed S.D.S. (Socialist Student Union) were raided. This was followed by more violence in June, when thousands of students turned out to protest the visit of the Shah and Empress of Iran. Police reacted with unprecedented ferocity and a student, Benno Ohnesorg, was killed (the date of his death, June 2, provided the name for one of the Baader-Meinhof sub-groups).

Almost overnight, attitudes began to harden. Gudrun Ensslin, who was to be one of the founders of Baader-Meinhof, but was still, at this time, an evangelical pacifist, spoke of the emergence of a 'fascist state' in West Germany. 'Now that I have experienced reality,' she said, 'I cannot be a pacifist any longer.'

She was not without support. Rudi Dutschke, a student and contributor to *Konkret*, a Marxist paper funded from East Germany, declared at Ohnesorg's funeral that the West German state was 'tending towards fascism'. He was to go on to take a leading role in the Paris student riots in May 1968. One of Dutschke's colleagues on *Konkret*, Ulrike Meinhof, like Gudrun Ensslin a pacifist, declared that Ohnesorg was a 'victim of S.S. mentality and practice'.

None of those destined to become leaders of the Baader-Meinhof gang were, as yet, known to each other. But the seeds were sown. Out of legitimate dissent grew the first fruits of a revolutionary fervour that was to lead, not to a vision of a new society, but to acts of indiscriminate and apparently senseless violence.

How this came about, given the high level of intelligence of almost every member of the gang, continues to baffle most political and social commentators. Ulrike Meinhof, daughter of a museum director, was educated at the Universities of Marburg and Münster; Gudrun Ensslin, daughter of a pastor in the Evangelical Church of Germany, read philosophy at the University of Tübingen and later enrolled for a doctorate at the Free University of West Berlin; Andreas Baader, son of an historian, had an indifferent school record, but made up in charm and sex appeal for what he lacked in education; Jan-Carl Raspe, son of a factory manager, studied at the Free University where he met Ulrike Meinhof, at the time a lecturer there; Ingrid Schubert, daughter of a wealthy businessman, was trained as a medical assistant; Thorwald and Astrid Proll, whose father was an architect, both studied at the Free University.

On this intellectual middle-class foundation, the Baader-Meinhof members built destruction. Such creed as they possessed seems, in the light of subsequent events, scarcely credible – to drive the German democratic state, forced to adopt an increasingly authoritarian position in answer to the terrorist attacks, further and further towards fascism. Only then, so the argument went, would the conditions be ripe for revolution.

From the start, then, the Baader-Meinhof gang was committed to violence. As early as 1968, Baader and his girl friend, Gudrun Ensslin, demonstrated their solidarity with other terrorist groups by planting an incendiary bomb in the Schneider department store in Frankfurt. They were assisted in this escapade by two other budding young terrorists, Horst Söhnlein and Thorwald Proll. The fire was put out without loss of life and the police successfully apprehended the culprits four days later.

This act of violence was seen by many of the nation's disaffected youth as showing the way out of the 'bourgeois trap'. A fire of a very different kind had been lit. It is still smouldering to this day.

One of the first to interview the arsonists in prison was Ulrike Meinhof. Although not yet ready to follow their actions, she wrote at the time, 'it is better to burn a department store than to run one'. Already she had espoused the anarchist cause. In less than a year she was to join forces with Baader and Ensslin and become herself a fugitive from justice.

On June 13, 1969, the four arsonists were let out of jail pending an appeal to be heard the following November. They were greeted by many radicals as heroes; comparisons were made with Angela Davis and Daniel Cohn-Bendit. Their following among students and radical sympathizers grew. One of their most ardent supporters was Ulrike Meinhof; another was Horst Mahler, legal champion of the Left and founder member of the 'Socialist Lawyers Collective'.

When their appeal was rejected, only one of the original four – Horst Söhnlein – gave himself up to the authorities. The other three immediately went underground where an extensive network of friends and sympathizers helped them to escape to France and thence to Switzerland. After three months, Baader and Ensslin felt confident enough to return to Germany. Baader was arrested in Berlin in the early hours of April 3, 1970, but Ensslin remained at large for a further two years, by which time the charges against her included – in addition to arson – robbery and complicity to murder.

In May, 1970. occurred the extraordinary event which brought the Baader-Meinhof gang into being. Sometime during Baader's imprisonment in the Tegel Prison in Berlin a plot was hatched which was to establish the pattern for later and equally daring attempts to spring terrorists from jail. The mastermind behind the plan was Horst Mahler, whose band of politically motivated lawyers had had, as yet, little chance to prove themselves. Mahler visited Baader frequently in prison, as did a woman styling herself Dr. Gretel Weitermeier, who was later established to have been Baader's girl friend, Gudrun Ensslin. Another visitor was Ulrike Meinhof who saw Baader five times between May 1 and May 14. None of these visits was monitored by the authorities, prisoner and visitor being allowed to speak freely and in private.

The first part of the escape plan involved Baader in the pretence of writing a book on the 'Organization of young people on the fringes of society'. To this end, permission was obtained for him to do research at the West German Institute for Social Questions in the quiet suburb of Dahlem. As it happened, Ulrike Meinhof, whose social-problem television stories had already earned her a certain notoriety, was a habituée of the Institute where much of her research was done. It thus came as no surprise to Frau Gertrud Lorenz, librarian on duty at the Institute, when, on the morning of Thursday, May 14, Frau Meinhof requested permission to work alongside the prisoner, Andreas Baader, whose book she had offered to help research.

While the library assistants were kept busy fetching books for the two 'researchers', the second part of the plan was put into action. Two young women – later established to have been Ingrid Schubert and Irene Goergens – were given permission to do research into therapy for juvenile criminals. They had hardly settled into their seats when the door bell rang again. This time it was a masked man (his identity has never been established) who wasted no time in preliminaries. Aided by Schubert and Goergens, both of whom produced

leaders (including Mahler himself) were arrested and imprisoned. It was not just escape plans that were hatched in consultations between lawyer and client; arms were smuggled into the prisoner's cell and crimes against life and property were masterminded from behind prison walls. In Ulrike Meinhof's words 'a few dozen fighters, who go into action without endless talk, can fundamentally change the political scene'.

There followed a series of violent bank raids for which the Baader-Meinhof gang claimed responsibility. On December 22, 1971, there was a raid on the Mortgage and Exchange Bank in Kaiserslautern, in the course of which a police officer was killed. Now the gang were wanted not just for arson, robbery and grievous bodily harm, but for first degree murder. Nor was it to stop there. Over the next seven years more than 20 people were to die as a result of Baader-Meinhof activities, scores were to be injured and the nation was to be held to ransom on four separate occasions. The trail of dead and injured alienated all but a lunatic fringe of society and so deprived the terrorists of their cherished status as martyrs. Not that it made any difference. As long as they believe in themselves as the legitimate scourge of a corrupt democracy the campaign of violence will continue.

After Mahler's arrest in October 1970 Andreas Baader took over his mantle as leader. Under his direction the gang began to devise a new strategy – the kidnapping of prominent people to be held as hostages against the release of imprisoned members of the gang. The strategy – which survived the arrest of the three ringleaders, Baader, Ensslin and Meinhof in 1972 – was not always successful. The Chief Federal Prosecutor, Dr. Siegfried Buback, the President of the West German Supreme Court, Günter von Drenkmann, the head of the Dresdner Bank, Herr Jürgen Ponto and the President of the West German Employers' Association, Hanns Martin Schleyer, have all been murdered. (Jürgen Ponto was shot by his own goddaughter, Susanne Albrecht). No terrorists were released in exchange for these 'prominent citizens'.

But the gang scored a notable success in February 1975 when Peter Lorenz, Chairman of the West Berlin Christian

Democrats, was kidnapped by the June 2 Movement. A letter setting out the kidnapper's demands was published in all the major national newspapers. 'If all demands are precisely met,' the letter stated, 'the safety of the prisoner Lorenz is guaranteed. Otherwise a consequence as in the case of Chief Justice Günter von Drenkmann is unavoidable.' The government knew the threat was serious. Six days after Lorenz's capture five terrorists were flown – in accordance with the kidnapper's instructions – from West Berlin to Frankfurt where a Boeing 707 was waiting to take them to Aden. Only then was Lorenz freed.

By 1975 most of the original members of the gang were in jail. Now only such extremists as the S.P.K. (Socialist Patients' Collective) continued to give the gang their active support. This group was founded by Dr. Wolfgang Huber of the Psychiatric-Neurological Clinic of Heidelberg University, who believed that an act of violence directed against the state could be instrumental in curing mental illness. 'There must be no therapeutic act which has not previously been clearly and uniquely shown to be a revolutionary act,' one of the group's manifestos declared. 'The system has "made us sick"! Let us strike the deathblow at the sick system.' So the Baader-Meinhof found an unexpected ally in Dr. Huber and his supporters and the acts of 'therapy' continued.

One of the members of the S.P.K. for whom such 'therapy' proved fatal was Siegfried Hausner, whose involvement with the Baader-Meinhof gang led to his death in a raid on the German Embassy in Stockholm in April 1975. He blew himself up with his own bomb. It was in his name that the kidnappers of Hanns Martin Schleyer demanded, in September 1977, the release of eleven terrorists held in jails in four different states in West Germany.

In May 1975, Ulrike Meinhof committed suicide in her cell in Stammheim Prison. She was not the first such casualty. On November 9, 1974, Holger Meins, one of the original members of the gang, died in prison as a result of a hunger strike. Both these deaths excited a flood of accusations from other members of the gang, speaking, as always, through their lawyers. But there can be no doubt the suicides were caused, not by the harshness of the authorities, but by the failure of those members of the gang still at large to secure their release. The same can be said of the suicides, in October and November 1977, of Andreas Baader, Jan-Carl Raspe, Gudrun Ensslin and Ingrid Schubert.

Despite the success of the police in tracking down almost all its original members, the Baader-Meinhof gang still exists. It has of necessity broken up into a number of splinter groups, called variously the R.A.F. (Red Army Faction), Baader-Meinhof, Haag-Mayer, Roter Morgen (Red Morning) and the June 2 Movement. But all the crimes committed under these names bear the unmistakeable stamp of Baader-Meinhof.

In the wake of the arrests following the killing of Hanns Martin Schleyer and the triumphant rescue at Mogadishu, it would seem the sting has been removed from the tail of the Baader-Meinhof gang and the groups it spawned. But the threats against life and property continue. One of these threats – to attack Lufthansa planes with ground-to-air rockets – had immediate impact: pilots were told to make random changes in direction in take-off and landing, and bookings nosedived. Even without its original leaders, Baader-Meinhof is still a force to be reckoned with.

3. THE SCHLEYER AFFAIR

THE CRIME

After the kidnapping, when police were trying to work out what happened, they were able to pick out a number of small incidents which were later to prove highly significant:

- On July 6, 1977, a young man entered an economics institute in Hamburg. Politely, he showed his student pass and asked for information on 'Messrs. Ponto and Schleyer' – 'I'm writing a doctorate on leading personalities in economics,' he said. The staff put some papers together. The next day, the young man arrived and went into the reading room on the second floor to study these papers.
- On July 25, a young man bought a white VW bus, registration K-C 3849, from a Cologne car dealer. In the sale document the young man gave his name as Peter Borke and his address as Cologne 1, Luxemburger Street, 521.
- On July 27, a 'Lisa Ries' rented a small apartment (No. 2065) on the sixth floor of a Cologne apartment block, Wiener Weg 1. The apartment had an allotted space – No. 127 – in the basement garage.
- On July 30, an electrical engineer, Arno Last, who lived in the Cologne suburb of Porz had his yellow 300D Mercedes stolen. It was a new car, equipped with a tow-bar. The theft was a routine case which did not even appear in the local press.

- On August 3, the caretaker of the Cologne apartment block at Wiener Weg 1, Friedrich Wilk, returned early from a holiday on the Baltic. Checking up on the basement garage, Wilk discovered a car that was unknown to him, a new yellow 300D Mercedes with a tow-bar. Wilk took down the number and blocked the car's exit. In the evening, two young men, who said they were the owners of the Mercedes, rang at his door. They asked him to clear the exit. Wilk wanted to know what they meant by putting their car there in the first place. One of the two, a young man with gold-rimmed glasses, said he was the fiancé of Fräulein Ries in apartment 2065. Wilk, mollified, cleared the exit and the Mercedes was driven out. Later, it was returned. Wilk didn't bother with it again.
- A few days later, Wilk met Fräulein Ries. He described her as in her middle twenties, with shoulder-length blonde hair. She asked to have the key to her letter box. Handing over the key, Wilk got a quick look at her apartment. It was not yet furnished. There was nothing in it except some yellow curtains.
- On the morning of September 5, Wilk went down to inspect the basement garage. In parking space No. 127 stood the Mercedes. It had not been taken out for several days. Beside it, there was an unfamiliar white VW bus. The side and back windows were hung with yellow curtains. Inside Wilk could see a blue pram. Clearly, the bus belonged to a young married couple in the block of flats. Wilk scribbled down the number – K-C 3849 – on a piece of paper and made a mental note to make enquiries about it among the tenants.

That afternoon, Hanns Martin Schleyer was kidnapped. The gang used the yellow Mercedes and the white VW bus.

It was not by any means a totally unexpected attack. A month before, Schleyer had been called up in his holiday house in Meersburg by the Interior Minister, Werner Maihofer, who informed him that, in the opinion of his Ministry and the German Criminal Office, Schleyer had become one of the most 'at-risk' people in Germany.

On August 10, Cologne police had discussed Schleyer's security with a delegation from the two national organizations of which Schleyer was a leading member – the Confederation of German Industry and the Federation of German Employers. The Cologne police chief, Heinz Darius, announced that Schleyer's security status had been upgraded. He already had official security at his family house in Stuttgart. Now he was placed at 'risk-level No. 1'. Security would be provided at his places of work in Stuttgart and Cologne and his Cologne residence. When on the premises, the building would be visited three times an hour; in his absence, once an hour.

The decision to raise Schleyer to the status of 'risk-level No. 1' was taken for several good reasons.

Firstly, he was an important public figure. As President of the Federation of German Employers, he was on the advisory board of 17 corporations. The Confederation of German Industry, of which he was President, is the parent organization of 95,000 firms, employing altogether eight million people. He was also on the board of Daimler-Benz.

Secondly, his image made him a natural target for radicals for other reasons. He was a beefy man with a face marked by duelling-scars, who in TV broadcasts seemed to radiate sternness and impatience. He seemed the very prototype of the exploiter. He was a staunch Christian Democrat, honorary consul for Brazil (where murder and torture are seen as legitimate means for the defence of the business order), and the force behind the shutting-out of 420,000 metal workers in Baden-Württemberg in 1963. He was also a former S.S. officer, responsible for coordinating industry in part of Nazi-occupied Czechoslovakia. In short, for any would-be kidnapper he was a veritable Frankenstein of capitalism – an image that was both gross and unfair, as both the police and the government were to discover.

Thirdly, he was probably already on the terrorists' list. When the terrorist lawyer, Siegfried Haag, was arrested on November 30, 1976, police found a mass of papers which were incriminating, but all too often enigmatic. In one case, decipherment came too late. There was a reference to a planned assassination attempt code-named 'Margarine'. In the Federal Criminal Office, Police President, Horst Herold and the Federal Prosecutor, Siegfried Buback, had both tried to guess what the word meant. Only when Buback was murdered in Karlsruhe on April 7, 1977, did the police investigators have their answer: there is a German margarine called 'SB' – the initials of Siegfried Buback.

A second message in the Haag papers ran: *'big money hm auschecken. diskutieren, wo den typ bunkern. big rausholе,'* which means roughly: 'Check out hm big money. Discuss where to hide the guy. Big pickings.' Who was 'H.M.'? One possibility was Hanns Martin Schleyer.

Two further events in the summer of 1977 seemed to show that the police were right to regard Schleyer as a likely victim. After the murder of Jürgen Ponto, Chairman of the Dresdner Bank, on July 30, 1977, employees at the Hamburg economics institute identified the young man who at the beginning of July had asked for papers on Ponto and Schleyer. The papers had been given to Willy Peter Stoll, 27, who had once worked in the office of the terrorist lawyer, Klaus Croissant.

Although no one knew it until later, Willy Peter Stoll was also the polite young man with the gold-rimmed glasses who had pretended to be the 'fiancé of Fräulein Ries'. Lisa Ries was in reality Friederike Krabbe, 27. Her pseudonym was suggested by the name of one of Schleyer's former Nazi associates, Fritz Ries.

The second event occurred on August 15. Stuttgart police raided the apartment of a former nurse, Gabriele Heim, who had been connected with the terrorist lawyers, Croissant and Armin Newerla. In her apartment the police found video-tapes which included scenes of Chancellor Schmidt's annual summer festival in Bonn on July 1. The film showed a host of prominent personalities from the worlds of politics and business. On the film, a young man had made sardonic comments like: 'We will have to look at these ones a bit more closely.' Clearly, any top businessman was a potential victim. The voice was later identified as that of a Munich actor, Christoph Wackernagel.

Schleyer soon discovered what it meant to be on 'risk-level No. 1'. On Wednesday, August 17, three days after returning from holiday, he flew to Cologne to work at his second office at the headquarters of the Employers' Federation. On the same day, at 5.00 p.m. the Cologne police arrived at his apartment, on the second floor of a four-storey house at Raschdorffstrasse, 10. He was advised to put in a wide-angled peep hole in the door, a second lock and three emergency buttons – by the door, by the bed and in the living room.

At midday the following day, the 18th, detectives visited Schleyer in his office. Schleyer's rooms could be overlooked from a street that ran along the Rhine, and on police orders heavy curtains were hung that same afternoon. In addition, Schleyer was to have a guard set behind bullet-proof doors to screen visitors, and an electronic surveillance system. The vehicle in which Schleyer's bodyguards travelled was given a radio call sign: 'Uran'. The officials were told to communicate with the central police station of Cologne using the prefix '*Zweig*' ('Branch'). If Schleyer was on his way home, the guards might for example radio '*Zweig* 20', which meant that Schleyer was to be in his apartment from 8.00 p.m. His name was removed from his bell and his letter box. Similar precautions were taken in Stuttgart, at the headquarters of Daimler-Benz.

Schleyer did not seem affected by the measures. Talk of kidnapping was anyway taboo in the Schleyer household. Even the murder of Jürgen Ponto, a family friend, was not mentioned. When at the end of August, Schleyer met Peter Lorenz, who had been abducted two years previously by the June 2 Movement, kidnapping was hardly mentioned. Schleyer noticed Lorenz's two security men and remarked in passing: 'Yes, now they've given me some of those.'

In mid-August, Schleyer acquired three police bodyguards – Roland Pieler, who was just 20, 24-year-old Helmut Ulmer and Reinhold Brändle, 41.

Pieler, the oldest of a family of five was, to put it kindly, a slow developer. He liked to read Mickey Mouse books and motor cycle brochures (he had a Honda 500). When he left secondary school at 16, his ambition, according to a questionnaire, was to join the 'F.B.I.'. His mother,

Elisabeth, was surprised and a little shocked: 'I can't understand it,' she said, 'Roland's not a violent person.'

Roland enjoyed his profession. During his two-year training in Göppingen, he took private lessons in judo, and at home he used to practise shooting with an air-pistol. He was soon reckoned a crack-shot. On March 23, 1977, one day after his 20th birthday, he was promoted detective constable.

When Roland was given the Schleyer job, it seemed to promise to be good fun. One evening, he was invited to have a drink in Schleyer's house. He stayed there until 1.00 a.m.

On the Sunday before his death, September 4, Roland went with his parents and his 16-year-old girlfriend, Heike Finke, to the sports ground at Waiblingen, near Stuttgart. Roland's favourite sister, Petra, was playing in the finals of a local handball championship. He had arranged to meet his two comrades, Ulmer and Brändle, at 3.30 p.m. and drive on to Cologne in a police Mercedes. Schleyer was due to fly up from Stuttgart early the next day. Roland told his mother to get some money out of the bank for him so that he could go on holiday to Ireland one week later. He was a little uneasy, or so it now seems with hindsight. Before leaving, he said lightly: 'Let's hope nothing happens.' And Heike remembered later: 'He wasn't too keen on going. He said he had a feeling that this time something was going to go wrong.'

Helmut Ulmer, a hulking 6′ $2\frac{1}{2}$″, weighing 192 lbs, had studied electrical engineering. In his spare time he raised rabbits; in Enzweihingen, his home town near Stuttgart, he was the secretary of a local club for breeding small animals. Drinking coffee after lunch that Sunday, he told his parents a bit more about his job. He described how, when driving, he always had his pistol on his lap and a sub-machine gun in front of him on the floor. Then he was busy with his rabbits until it was time for him to go.

Sergeant Reinhold Brändle had been divorced from his wife, Inge, some years before. Their son, 12-year-old Oliver, had spent the weekend with him, as usual when his father was not on duty. Brändle had been a policeman since 1956, and for the last eleven years had been in the motor-cycle unit. He was the trainer of a local schoolboys' football team. His son Oliver was goalie. When he dropped off the boy at his mother's, he said he would be going with Schleyer to Sweden. He said he would bring Oliver a present and added that he liked his new job because it involved a good deal of travel.

On Monday, September 5, Schleyer got up early, about 5.00 a.m. His house in Stuttgart was a plain, two-storey family house, with three bedrooms upstairs, and a living room, dining room and kitchen downstairs. He had no breakfast. The others were still asleep. Eric Meyer, his Stuttgart chauffeur, drove up in a Daimler-Benz 450, and the two men set out for the airport. No-one in the family saw him go.

At 6.30 a.m., Schleyer took off for Cologne in the twin-engined company jet, a Daimler-Falcon. One hour later, his Cologne driver, Heinz Marcisz, picked him up. Since the killing of Buback, the 41-year-old Marcisz had been frequently pestered by his wife to look for another job – it was too dangerous, she said, to drive so important a man. He would answer in an off-hand way: 'What does it matter how I go? Whether I fall down stairs or whether they shoot me up – it's all the same.'

That morning Marcisz drove Schleyer directly to the Employers' Federation headquarters, on Oberländer Ufer. A cup of coffee, the post, then 'morning-prayers' – a regular Monday-morning review of the economic situation with specialist reporters. After lunch at 2.00 p.m., a meeting with employers from the metal industry. In the evening, Schleyer was due in Düsseldorf for a speech on opinion-polls and the following morning in Stockholm for a meeting of the Swedish employers.

At his home in Stuttgart that morning, Schleyer's youngest son, Jörg, a lanky 23-year-old, breakfasted with his mother, Waltrude. Jörg, studying politics and modern history at Munich, planned to become a journalist. Later, Jörg went shopping with his mother. At mid-day, they met friends in the pedestrian precinct of the Stuttgart Centre and went with them for a coffee. At 2.00 p.m. Jörg and his mother returned home. Waltrude cleared up, arranged some flowers and gave some instructions to the housemaid. At 4.00 p.m.

Jörg and Waltrude had a cup of coffee together.

The same day, in Münster, top police officers began a four-day conference on terrorism. Chancellor Helmut Schmidt was to be one of the speakers. The Federal Criminal Office had put together some statistics for the conference on recent burglaries. Between January 1 and June 30, thieves had taken, among other things, about 600 sets of identification papers; 226 blank passports; 456 blank driving licences; 346 official seals and stamps; 2,040 hand guns; 1,463 rifles; 197 sub-machine guns; 15 hand grenades; and 20 radios of the type used by the German security forces.

At 5.10 p.m. Cologne's police headquarters picked up a short coded message from Schleyer's escort: '*Zweig* 17.30'. Schleyer would be back at his Cologne apartment at Raschdorffstrasse 10 at 5.30 p.m. No particular precautions were necessary. As per routine, a radio patrol car, Arnold 14/14, was despatched to Raschdorffstrasse.

If things had not gone wrong, everything would have seemed merely routine. As it was, the questions afterwards were endless. Should the weapon stores and passport offices have been better guarded? Were Schleyer's bodyguards sufficiently prepared for their duties? Should a 20-year-old who liked to read Mickey Mouse comics have been a bodyguard? Should Schleyer's car and his bodyguards' car have been armoured? Was it sensible to put all three members of the police-escort in one car? Should the police have warned caretakers to report rentals by young people who then never moved in? Certainly, much more could have been done; but equally, however much was done, there could still have been weak links, impossible to spot in advance.

At 5.28 p.m. Schleyer's two-car convoy turned into the Vincenz-Statz Street, a tree-lined, one-way road in Cologne's Braunsfelder suburb, running parallel to Raschdorffstrasse where Schleyer lived. On the left, stood a white VW bus. Suddenly, from the same side of the street, a yellow Mercedes swerved in front of the convoy and came to rest diagonally across the road, its front on the right-hand pavement. Simultaneously a blue pram rolled out from the left into the path of Schleyer's car. Marcisz braked, swerved towards the Mercedes and slammed to a halt. The escort car, with a screech of tyres, struck the leading car from behind.

Five people standing well back on the pavements swung round with sub-machine guns and opened fire. Bullets scythed through the windshield, side windows and rear windows of the escort car at head height. Two of the policemen had time to shoot back. Ulmer fired eight shots from his sub-machine gun and Pieler fired three pistol shots. None of the bullets hit their mark. Brändle fell with 20 wounds, at least two of which would have been immediately fatal. Ulmer died with three bullet wounds in the head. Eight bullets passed clean through Pieler's body.

Schleyer, sitting in the back of the leading Mercedes, was dragged out of the car by the gangsters and pushed towards the VW bus. Marcisz threw open his door to help his boss. The terrorists, who had at first ignored Marcisz, opened up on him. One bullet tore open a main artery and Marcisz began to bleed to death. Schleyer had, meanwhile, been shoved inside the bus. The other terrorists leapt in. The bus roared off. The whole thing took just three minutes.

The only eye-witness was a 10-year-old, Andreas Geyr, son of a lawyer living in the street. A neighbour opened a window and shouted to him: 'Come on in quickly; they're making a film here.'

At 5.33 p.m. the police got a call from Vincenz-Statz Street: 'People are shooting each other with machine guns,' shouted an unidentified voice, 'there are many dead and wounded.' At once the radio patrol car, which was on its way to Raschdorffstrasse, was ordered to the scene, along with a second car.

Meanwhile, a man driving a BMW had, on his own initiative, set off in pursuit of the fleeing VW bus. A few blocks down the road, a Belgian army lorry suddenly swung across the street behind the VW but in front of the BMW. The driver, unaware of what was going on, was turning round. As the lorry pulled clear, the BMW driver saw one of the patrol cars, waved it down and shouted: 'The car you're looking for is heading for the autobahn!'

The patrol car turned and sped towards the nearest autobahn exit, but the police never got a sight of the fugitives.

At headquarters, the police put out a news flash that Schleyer had been kidnapped.

At 5.50 p.m. in the Schleyer house in Stuttgart, *Bild*, the mass-circulation tabloid, called. Jörg picked up the phone. The *Bild* man asked: 'Have you heard anything about a bomb attack on your father?' Of course, Jörg hadn't. Worried, he went outside and asked the two police on watch. They knew nothing either, but radioed their headquarters in Stuttgart. No news. Jörg went back inside. He did not think it necessary to call his mother, who was clearing up upstairs.

Five minutes later, *Time* Magazine called up from Bonn, and asked: 'Has there been an attempt on your father's life?' At 6.05 p.m. *Bild* phoned again. This time it was not a question but a piece of information: 'There has been an attempt on your father's life in Cologne. Four people are dead. Whether your father is among the dead or not we don't know.'

The repeated ringing of the telephone had attracted Frau Schleyer's attention. She came downstairs. Jörg told her what he had just heard. She said nothing, but slumped into an armchair and stared silently in front of her.

From now on, the telephone rang at ever briefer intervals. Jörg answered each call. Each time his mother asked 'What is it? Tell me. Is he dead? What's happened?'

At 6.30 p.m. a 20-man police squad surrounded the house. Jörg tried to reach his father at the Employers' Federation headquarters in Cologne. There was no-one there except a porter who told him only that his father had left the building at 5.00 p.m.

At 7.00 p.m. the South German Television news confirmed the attack. Police rigged up a telephone-tap in the Schleyer's house in hopes of intercepting a blackmail call.

Half an hour later, Jörg's 32-year-old brother, Hanns-Eberhard, a lawyer in Stuttgart, arrived at the Schleyer house. Towards 9.00 p.m., 28-year-old Arndt Schleyer, a junior barrister in Heidelberg, arrived. Now all the family was there except for Dirk, a 25-year-old student on holiday on the Greek island of Aegina with his girlfriend. (It took three days for the German Embassy in Athens to contact him.) There was no further news that night. The only government official to call was the Economics Minister, Friderichs. At 4.00 a.m. the family went to bed.

At Roland Pieler's white terraced home in Albert-Schweitzer Street in Hochdorf, near Reichenbach, 40 miles south-west of Stuttgart, Roland's mother turned on the radio shortly after 7.00 p.m. The news was already running. She heard only '... surprise attack on Hanns Martin Schleyer.' She switched the radio off at once and just had time to say to her husband: 'Switch on the TV' when the telephone went. It was Roland's grandmother: 'Have you heard?' she said, 'Roland was in it!' The Pielers called the local police. They knew nothing.

Then Frau Pieler called Roland's girlfriend, Heike, in Reichenbach. Heike's father, Hans, was celebrating his 48th birthday. Heike thought it must be Roland himself ringing. He usually called in when he was away on a job. 'I'll give him an earful,' she thought, 'keeping me waiting like this.'

But it wasn't Roland; it was Frau Pieler, She sobbed: 'Heike, I think something has happened to our Roland.' Heike began to cry. Her mother came to the phone, took the receiver and tried to reassure Frau Pieler: 'It's Hans's birthday. *Of course* nothing's happened.'

At 8.00 p.m. Heike and her parents watched the news together. They saw some film taken at the scene of the crime. Heike thought she recognized Roland. The Finkes called Frau Pieler to tell her so. But shortly afterwards, two policemen from Esslingen brought Frau Pieler the news of her son's death. A doctor was called to administer a tranquilizer. Frau Pieler called Heike and told her what had happened.

In Enzweihingen, the local police chief brought Eugen Ulmer the news of the death of his only son. Frau Brändle learnt of the attack from the television.

In Cologne's Vincenz-Statz Street the police had been able to do nothing for the four men. A rescue helicopter circling above and ambulances with blue lights flashing and sirens wailing all withdrew uselessly. The dead were covered with plastic sheeting. They lay there in the gathering gloom caught in the beams of two powerful spot lights.

Meanwhile, the terrorists' Mercedes had been identified. It was the one that had been stolen on July 30 in Porz. The registration of the VW bus had been established by the BMW driver: K-C 3849.

At Wiener Weg 1, Herr Wilk, the caretaker, was listening to the news. When he heard that number, he remembered the strange VW bus with the blue pram which had stood in the basement garage. He took out the scrap of paper which he had been carrying in his breast pocket and compared the two numbers. They were the same. Wilk immediately called the police who appeared towards 8.00 p.m. They found the white VW bus back in its spot in the basement. The police feared it might be booby trapped. An explosives expert was brought in. Safely hidden behind the projection of a wall, he opened the VW's door with a rope.

Inside, the investigators found a photocopied letter from the terrorists to the government. (Terrorists work with photocopies to prevent analysis of the paper and the handwriting.) The note demanded that the government avoid all public search measures 'or we shoot Schleyer immediately without talking about terms for his release.' The letter, the contents of which were not immediately made public, was signed 'Commando Siegfried Hausner R.A.F.' (a reference to the terrorist who had blown himself up during the attack on the German Embassy in Stockholm).

Towards midnight, the apartment of 'Lisa Ries', alias Friederike Krabbe, was forced open. It was empty. The only things left behind were an air mattress, a walkie-talkie, a chair and a small bedside lamp.

In the Vincenz-Statz Street in Braunsfeld, every square centimetre was being searched for clues. In the blue pram, police found a baby's toy – an orange bird with a white teething ring, two pairs of rally gloves and a Wilson tennis racket in a blue-and-white cover.

On the basis of the spent ammunition found at the scene – some 300 shots were found in all – police were able to list the terrorists' weapons: a 12-mm Colt, a Swiss automatic of 5.6-mm calibre (the same type of weapon used in the Buback and Ponto killings), a number of 9-mm sub-machine guns and some shotguns.

At one point the police were interrupted when Anni Marcisz, wife of Schleyer's chauffeur, arrived at the scene. A policeman led her over to her husband's corpse, where she broke down. The police worked at the scene of the crime until 3.00 a.m. Only then were the Mercedes shoved into three furniture vans and taken to the Criminal Office headquarters in Wiesbaden.

Ten hours after the attack, the street was handed over to the cleaners. The corpses of the three bodyguards and the driver were put into coffins and taken away.

By the time the morning sun began to shine through the hawthorn trees, and the first locals passed by muttering about the need for 'a new Hitler', all traces of the crime had vanished.

In Bonn, Schmidt, who had been informed of the attack by the police at about 6.00 p.m., immediately took over the leadership of the hunt for Schleyer's kidnappers, a role that he was not to abandon for another seven weeks. His first task was to make a television statement. At 9.20 p.m., the Chancellor went into the Bonn studios of A.R.D.-TV.

In his statement, Schmidt addressed the terrorists directly: 'While I am speaking, no doubt the criminals are listening in. They may be experiencing a feeling of power and triumph. But they should not be deceived. Terrorism has no chance in the long run. For against terrorism stand the wills of the state and of the whole people.'

Yet for the next few weeks, it was not the Chancellor who dominated West Germany's political life; it was the Red Army Faction.

THE SEARCH

From now on the Federal Republic was a different state. Not only the police and the Criminal Office were brought in, but also the Secret Service, normally limited to foreign activities, and the Intelligence Service, which was legally supposed to operate only within the armed forces.

Road blocks were set up by the police, who stopped thousands of drivers to see their papers and to search their cars with a rigorousness normally reserved only for those going into East Germany.

Opposition to such infringements of individual freedom was scant. When, at a meeting on security between politicians and officials in Bonn, Munich's Police President, Manfred Schreiber, indicated that there was 'no basis in law' for such actions, the news was received with a few shrugs. A law would simply have to be made that sanctioned the necessary measures.

Daily, government and opposition debated new laws. The conservatives wanted to make telephone tapping easier, to supervise discussions between lawyers and arrested terrorists and to clamp down further on demonstrations. Measures were passed to allow meetings between imprisoned terrorists and their lawyers to be interrupted and terrorists to be totally isolated.

The state was on new ground. The kidnapping of the Berlin politician, Peter Lorenz, in February 1975 had, by comparison with the Schleyer case, been quite a light-hearted affair. Lorenz's driver was not shot, but driven off with a broom stick. The kidnappers made their demands known through a landlord who was also called Peter Lorenz. Lorenz himself described his kidnappers as 'really quite nice young people' with 'misplaced ideals'. Later, after his release, he recalled that they had mended his long underpants, which had been torn during the struggle. Even the killings of Buback and Ponto did not have such severe consequences. They were over immediately and demanded no political action.

Now however the state, in adopting a firm line, was forced to remodel itself in response to the demands of a handful of trigger-happy gangsters. The head of the government of one of the greatest industrial nations on earth had to negotiate as an equal with a Mafia of young killers, who no longer even attempted to give themselves the veneer of legitimacy.

All this arose from the government's decision to hold firm. To give in would almost certainly have guaranteed further assaults in the future.

The man with the task of freeing the state from its ignominious role as the blackmailed party was the head of the Federal Criminal Office, Police President, Horst Herold. He was on holiday in the southern German Alps when the news broke. He immediately drove to Wiesbaden and took a night flight by helicopter to Bonn. The 54-year-old Herold had already made a name for himself before he took over the leadership of the Criminal Office in 1971. In the Criminal Office headquarters in Wiesbaden, he had installed a computer into which all criminal police information was fed. Data could be recalled in seconds from 800 terminals at frontier posts, police stations, and even specially equipped patrol cars. This innovation earned Herold, a tubby man who always carried a revolver on his hip, even when he wore civilian clothes, the nickname 'Mr Computer'.

Herold needed data to feed into his electronic toy in Wiesbaden, but the information could only be provided by the kidnappers themselves. With this in mind, Herold's basic concept, devised in conjunction with the Chancellor, was to delay – to spin out replies, to work out ways of winning yet more time. In this way, he hoped, details could be collected which would build mosaics of the criminals' characters and perhaps even give an indication of their hiding place. (The first consequence of this policy was that the terrorists' first letter, left in the VW bus, was not made public.)

The next day – Tuesday, September 6 – at 3.00 p.m., in the vicarage near the Protestant Church in Wiesbaden, Lehrstrasse 8, the telephone rang. The Dean's daughter, 12-year-old Bettina Neuschäfer, answered. Her father was in the church preparing for a service. When she said: 'Hello,' nobody replied. She heard a click: the caller had hung up. A little later she discovered a large, white, blank envelope in the letter-box. She took it out and put it on the table for her father.

The Dean returned shortly afterwards and found the letter. He opened it. Inside was a second envelope, also white. It bore the typewritten address: 'To the Federal Government.' Inside was a three page letter, also typewritten. On the letter-head was the emblem of the R.A.F., 'a sort of a drawing with a star and a sub-machine gun,' as he later described it. Also in the letter was a polaroid colour photo of Hanns Martin Schleyer. He was sitting under the R.A.F. emblem, wearing a dark-red track-suit top with a blue collar and blue bands on the sleeves. In his hand he held a notice: '6.9.77 Prisoner of the R.A.F.' Finally, there was a short handwritten note from Schleyer himself.

As Dean Neuschäfer was reading the letter, the telephone went. Without any preamble a woman's voice said in unaccented German: 'This is the Red Army Faction. In your letter-box you will find a message to the Federal Government.' Then the woman hung up. The Dean immediately informed the Criminal Office. Police arrived a few minutes later and took the letter by special police car to Herold's desk.

The note, written without capitals, read as follows:

'on monday 5.9.77 the siegfried hausner commando took prisoner the president of the employers federation and the confederation of german industry, hanns martin schleyer.

as a condition of his release we will repeat yet again our first communication to the federal government which, as has become known to us, has since yesterday been suppressed by the security forces.

that is the immediate secession of all search measures – or schleyer will be shot immediately. as soon as the search stops schleyer will be freed under the following conditions:

1. the r.a.f. prisoners
   andreas baader
   gundrun ensslin
   jan-carl raspe
   verena becker
   werner hoppe
   karl heinz dellwo
   hanna krabbe
   bernd rösner
   ingrid schubert
   irmgard möller

will be released in exchange for schleyer and allowed to travel to a country of their choice. günter sonnenberg, who because of his gunshot wound is in no condition to be under arrest, will be released immediately. the warrant for his arrest will be nullified. günter will leave with the ten prisoners with whom he should be immediately placed and allowed to speak,

2. the prisoners are to be brought to frankfurt airport before 8.00 a.m. on wednesday morning. before their departure at 12.00 they will be allowed to speak together at any time without any restrictions. at 10.00 a.m. one of the prisoners will announce to the commandos directly on german television the correct departure time of their flight.

3. as a control and guarantee for the lives of the prisoners until they have landed and been picked up, the prisoners should – at our suggestion – be accompanied by payot, the general secretary of the international federation for human rights at the u.n., and rev. niemöller [Martin Niemöller, anti-Nazi theologian and pacifist]. we ask them to take on this task so that the prisoners may land where they want.

naturally we would also agree to an alternative suggestion by the prisoners.

4. each of the prisoners will be given 100,000 deutschmarks.

5. this statement, which schleyer's photo and his letter prove to be authentic, will be made public this evening on the 8.00 p.m. news, uncut and unaltered.

6. we will announce a timetable for schleyer's release as soon as the release of the prisoners is confirmed, to avoid a statement by the federal government that they have been released when in fact no release has been effected.

we proceed on the basis that schmidt having demonstrated in stockholm how rapidly his decision fails, will do his best to clarify rapidly his relationship with this fat magnate of the national business cream.

dated 6.9.77

commando siegfried hausner

'r.a.f.'

The appended handwritten note from Schleyer was brief:

'They have told me that to continue the search will threaten my life. The same is true if the demands are not met and the ultimatum not complied with.

'I am well so far. I am uninjured and believe that I will be set free when the conditions are met.

'That however is not my decision.'

Both notes were photocopies. Only Schleyer's signature was original.

The most politically interesting part of the letter was the reference to the 'fat magnate of the national business cream,' which reveals the attitudes of many so-called 'social revolutionaries'. According to them, the true ruler of West Germany was the boss of all the bosses, the President of the Employers' Federation, Hanns Martin Schleyer. By kidnapping him, they hoped to demonstrate Schmidt's reliance on him.

The letter also gave a clue to the internal structure of the R.A.F. Among the names of those who should be released, there is no mention of the lawyer, Siegfried Gottlieb Haag, arrested in November 1976, nor of his associate Roland Mayer, since held in Bochum. Haag was, at the time of Schleyer's arrest, generally held to be the intellectual leader of the gang. Clearly, if he had been once, he now no longer was, perhaps because he was arrested without a weapon in his hand, and perhaps also because his arrest led to the capture of a mass of papers giving the names of members, addresses and a list of activities from the Buback murder to the Schleyer kidnapping (although all were in code).

The delaying tactics decided upon by the Criminal Office could only be put into effect after a meeting of the 'crisis staff' at 11.00 p.m. on Monday. The 'crisis staff' is an organization not covered by any article of the Constitution, any Federal law or standing order and yet, since the abduction of Lorenz in February 1975, it has become a firm institution in Bonn. It groups the most important cabinet ministers, representatives of the four parties and, as the need arises, the Minister-Presidents (the leaders of individual *Länder*, or provinces).

The authority of the crisis staff arose according to the needs of the hour. It overrode party squabbles and was thus a remarkable expression of democratic unity. As one conservative member said on the day after Schleyer's abduction: 'our task in opposition is now to establish clearly our joint responsibility with the government.'

That joint responsibility was established immediately. On the Monday evening, shortly after the attack, Opposition leader, Helmut Kohl was sitting in his Parliamentary office with some of his staff, when the door burst open. It was Schmidt. The Chancellor stormed in and said without more ado: 'Herr Kohl, I have to see you alone.' Kohl's colleagues vanished. Ten minutes later, Schmidt and Kohl had agreed in principle on a hard line and a policy of delay.

At 10.00 p.m. the first cars began to arrive for the crisis meeting. Many got their first impression of 'Fortress Bonn', already interwoven by almost four miles of barbed wire. Ministers drove up in bullet-proof cars. Men of the elite Frontier Force stood on guard, fingers on triggers.

The crisis staff met until 1.00 a.m. Among those present was the Chairman of the Daimler-Benz Board, Joachim Zahn, who said his company was ready to pay any sum demanded. It was the second time one of Mercedes' senior officials had been kidnapped. In 1975 the Montoneros, Argentinian urban guerrillas, kidnapped the production manager of Mercedes-Benz in Argentina, Heinrich Metz. The company had paid 7.5 million dollars to free him.

Schmidt did not even try to conceal his anger. He had, he said. 'heard too much nonsense.' He expressed indignation that the security organizations, with their ever increasing budgets (since 1975, the budget of the Office for the Protection of the Constitution increased from 75 to 90 million marks), still had no firm information on the nature of the new generation of terrorists. The crisis staff finally agreed that they should work to gain time and that there should be no question of an exchange of views over television. There was to be a news embargo.

In fact, Schmidt was being a little hard on the police – the terrorists were not as unknown as all that. After the murders of Buback and Ponto and other crimes, police found clues which enabled them to draw some conclusions about Schleyer's kidnappers.

The hard core of the Red Army Faction contained some 30 or 40 terrorists, who lived completely underground, communicating in the most secret ways, committed to a formerly unknown level of brutality. They had no direct contact with those who helped them to get cars, organize weapons or provide papers. Communication was only through middlemen, or sometimes by telephone. As Gerhard Boeden, Chief of the Anti-Terror Unit in the Criminal Office, said of the go-betweens: 'They get one task and see that through. Only then do they get another. Often they don't know why they have to do it.'

Methods of recruitment were also known. In the jargon of the group, 'the first principle of the R.A.F.' was that new members were only accepted into the hard core after months of testing. It was essential that the new recruit had already been tested in action.

They were not only ruthless; they were extraordinarily well organized. Herold told the crisis staff: 'Their scholastic accreditations, personal documents and driving licences are all in order.' Gone are the days when terrorists used stolen papers with made-up names, for any stolen or lost papers were immediately put on to the Wiesbaden computer, from where they could be spewed out at any time to any control point.

The Haag documents gave a particularly good insight into their organization. One paper was an accurate plan of action, a timetable that divided up the month of November among eleven terrorists. For example, on November 20, 'Michael', who was identified by the authorities as Haag's companion, Roland Mayer, was to *'Auto k' – 'Auto kaufen'* ('Buy a car'). 'Bodo' and 'Hans' had free days, but who these two were has yet to be discovered. 'Tim' was supposed to be in a *'Klotz'* – slang for high-rise building. 'Ede', later identified as Haag himself, also had a day off.

There were other indications too that further investigation might be rewarding. In May 1977, when Verena Becker was arrested, papers in her possession talked about an R.A.F. base which was 'probably in Alsace'. It was in Mulhouse, Alsace, that Schleyer was later found killed. And when, in April 1977, the German anarchist, Norbert Kröcher, was arrested in Sweden – Kröcher had planned the abduction of the former Swedish Minister of Foreign Affairs, Anna-Greta Leijon – a number of clues about underground tactics were found on him. There were instructions, for example, on intercepting police messages, on protection against bugs, on testing whether mail had been opened or not, on encoding messages, on putting in radio devices, on transmitting radio messages, on armaments, on renting property and cars, and, in particular, on making attacks in residential suburbs. Terrorists were advised to study the life-style of intended victims – their way of life, car-journeys, walks, places of recreation (galleries, concerts, theatres, cinemas). 'A number of hiding-places must be prepared for the attackers after the assault,' ran the notes, 'the distance from the scene of the crime to the first hiding place should be one or two kilometres.' (The distance between the scene of the crime in Cologne and the basement garage in Wiener Weg 1 was three kilometres.) Other significant sections discussed the selection of an assault site in which the distances were small enough to allow for the use of pistols and machine-guns and where the victim's car would be travelling slowly or would be stationary. Nine pages concerned precautions against observation and telephone tapping. There were tips which proved of particular relevance to the Schleyer case – for instance: 'Telephone briefly, never more than two minutes', and 'Never call twice from the same telephone box.'

Most ironic of all, the investigators discovered that they had had the details of the Schleyer kidnapping in their hands all the time. On August 30, the terrorist lawyer, Armin Newerla, was arrested on strong suspicion of being involved in a criminal conspiracy. His car was taken away and searched. On September 5, in the upholstery of the back seat, police found a sheet of A4 paper on which were two diagrams no one could interpret. In the afternoon of September 5, came the attempt; then, suddenly, the sketches made sense. The first one represented the entrance to Schleyer's home; the second showed the shape of the streets in the Braunsfeld suburb through which Schleyer was to travel to his home.

The only chance the Criminal Office had in their battle with these highly intelligent, thoroughly trained, and well-organized opponents, lay in the concept defined by Herold and Schmidt – to win both time and information – in collaboration with a massive police operation.

All the resources the country could muster were mobilized. An army of detectives was put on the case, the leadership of which was given to the Anti-Terrorist Department of the Criminal Office, whose leader was Gerhard Boeden. A special unit was set up to make searches at frontiers, another unit to coordinate searches in the various *Länder*, on roads, at airports and railway stations. A third was responsible for reserves – additional manpower, preparation of public searches, the acquisition of cars, the production of posters.

In the Cologne Police Headquarters, there had for some time been a special commission grouping representatives from the Federal Criminal Office, the North-Rhine-Westphalian Criminal Office and the Cologne police. Normally 150 men staffed it; but on the first day of the Schleyer search the number rose to 800. The place soon looked like a battle-field. Everywhere there were maps of Cologne, for most of the officials did not know the area. New arrivals were told: 'If you see the Cathedral in front of you, you're travelling towards the centre. If the Cathedral's in your mirror, you're leaving.' Tables and field telephones littered the room and spilled over into the hallways. Maps of previous case histories were pinned to the curtains – someone must have hoped that a knowledge of established criminal habits would prove stronger than the Wiesbaden computer.

Some of the statistics of the search were staggering. In the next seven weeks, the staff processed 3,826 leads. The work was recorded in over 100 files which covered 50 feet of shelving. Participating in the search were 140 military intelligence personnel. They brought with them over 60 army vehicles. The Federal Intelligence Agency was also brought in. They placed taps on all 36 telephone links with Switzerland. Each link had 500 lines, which meant 18,000 lines to supervise in case the kidnappers called their go-between, Denis Payot, in Geneva. Another 497 public telephone booths in the Cologne area were also tapped. In addition, 3,000 police guards, detectives and frontier agents were sent to protect politicians believed to be in danger.

On September 7 the kidnappers sent another message to the government. Again, they used a churchman, this time in Mainz, as a go-between. The same pattern was repeated – a telephone call, in which the caller said nothing, to establish whether the contact-man was at home; then the secret posting of the documents in the letter-box; and finally a phone call with the information that the Red Army Faction had left a message for the government in the box. Again a woman spoke, as if delivering a formal communiqué.

So it happened that at 6.02 p.m. on the 7th, Pastor Friedrich Schuster of Mainz's Christchurch became the recipient of the first video-tape from the kidnappers, showing Schleyer in captivity; in addition, he received two handwritten notes from Schleyer and a typewritten letter from the R.A.F.

In their letter the kidnappers accused the Federal Government of delaying tactics to 'effect a military solution'. They demanded that such tactics end and that the video-tape should be transmitted over television.

The tape shows three scenes. In the first, Schleyer sends greetings to his family. 'Considering the circumstances, I am doing relatively well.' Then – this time in glasses – he reads out a newspaper article. In the third scene, he explains to the government that he believes the kidnappers will set him free when their demands are fulfilled.

The pattern was repeated that evening, at the home of a Mainz suffragen Bishop, Wolfgang Rolly, who received a tape. On the tape a number of questions about Schleyer's private life, formulated by the Criminal Office and broadcast over the radio, were answered correctly – proof that Schleyer was still alive.

The next day an express letter to the *Frankfurter Rundschau*, set a new ultimatum for the departure of the prisoners – midday on September 9.

During those first three days, the government had not given in significantly to the demands. To keep the terrorists calm, they had made one small concession: a small extract from the first letter with the list of names of those terrorists who were to be released, was published. The policy worked:

the deadline was extended several times.

To introduce another delaying tactic and to preserve secrecy, the police decided to use a go-between: the Geneva-based lawyer, Denis Payot, who had been mentioned by the terrorists themselves.

Who was Denis Payot? One thing he emphatically wasn't: a star lawyer with a wide-ranging reputation. He was not, as the kidnappers assumed, a U.N. official but simply President of the 'Swiss League for Human Rights'. His office lay in Geneva's Uhrmacherviertel (Clockmakers' Quarter) on the Boulevard Georges Favon.

Payot, 35, fair and curly-headed, put himself forward as a lawyer who was much in demand. He let drop that his fee from the Federal Government would be a minimum of 500,000 marks (about £125,000). In fact, after seven dramatic weeks, he came out of the business with a somewhat reduced income: a first instalment of 10,000 Swiss francs (£2,500), then another 50,000 (£12,500) and a final one of 120,000 (£30,000), expenses inclusive.

After Schleyer was killed, a top official did indeed say that 'Payot has always served us very correctly.' But when it was first decided that the Geneva lawyer was to be the go-between, there were considerable reservations – not without reason: Payot, as President for the 'Swiss League for Human Rights', had defended Palestinian interests in the Near East and at the instigation of Gudrun Ensslin's parents had signed one of the protests sent to the U.N. Human Rights Commission about the condition in which the R.A.F. prisoners were being held. He had already therefore, had close connections with German terrorists. In addition, Payot had a country house in Grenoble. On November 30, 1976, Haag called this house and talked directly with Payot. The terrorist lawyer, Croissant, also seemed to have been a guest there at the time Interpol was searching for him.

Ambivalence about Payot's affiliations remained. Once, police received information about a telephone conversation between Payot and the kidnappers in which he made fun of the government's delaying tactics and said that Bonn's official view that no country would take the R.A.F. prisoners if released, was wrong.

Again, during his term as intermediary, Payot issued an ambiguous warning through his closest legal associate, Philip Preti: 'if the Germans want to solve the problem with force, we will let slip some important information.' What did Preti mean? Preti told *Stern* that the terrorists had drugged Schleyer during the first few days and then let him blow his mouth off about leading personalities in politics and business. They then pooled his statements to make an 80-page dossier of his opinions on the German state. Preti said: 'If this dossier were made public, Schmidt would have to resign.' Whether there was anything in this or not, only time will tell.

On September 9, Herold called Payot for the first time and asked him to take on the job as intermediary. Payot immediately gave a press conference in which he publicly accepted the offer.

That day, the kidnappers called the Foreign Service of the German Press Agency in Cologne. They demanded that the Schleyer video-tape be played on South German Television before 7.00 p.m.; then they would be ready to talk to Payot in Geneva. The German Press Agency informed the Criminal Office. A conference followed: the police decided to stick to the hard line, a decision confirmed in a discussion between Herold and Schmidt.

The next day, September 10, at 11.25 a.m., a woman called up Payot and identified herself as an R.A.F. member. She gave instructions that before 6.00 p.m. the following day, the eleven R.A.F. members whose release had been demanded, should appear on German television to announce their departure. This deadline, like the others, was ignored.

On the same day, the dead policemen were buried in Stuttgart. Among the mourners was the 16-year-old girl friend of Roland Pieler, Heike Finke. She had previously seen Roland's body in the mortuary in Feuerbach. She derived some small comfort from the sight: 'Roland did not look so bad as the others. His right cheek was a little grazed, but otherwise there was nothing. The faces of the others looked awful.'

In Cologne, some townspeople nailed up pictures of the

three policemen and of Marcisz on a tree in Vincenz-Statz Street. They arranged fresh flowers against the base of the tree, laid a laurel wreath and lit candles. They wrote on a placard: 'To the victims of a perfidious murder.'

Down the street, the bell of the lawyer, Florian Geyr, at No. 12, rang. The house was just 50 yards from the scene of the attack and it was Geyr's 10-year-old son, Andreas, who had been the only eye-witness of the attack. Andreas' mother, 39-year-old Jutta, opened the door. Two young men stood there. Jutta asked: 'Are you from the police?'

'No.'

'Well, from the press then?'

'Something like that.'

She asked to see their papers. Then one said to the other: 'Come on we had better go.' They got on a heavy motorcycle and roared off down the street.

The family immediately called up the police. Jutta was certain that one, at least, of the young men was one of the wanted terrorists. Andreas was sent to live elsewhere until the fuss had died down. 'It would have been a disaster if the terrorists had taken the child as a hostage,' said one detective, Karl-Heinz Pöhler. 'We might just as well have packed up and gone home.'

Across town, some young people from Holland arrived at Wiener Weg 1, in which Friederike Krabbe, under the name 'Lisa Ries', had rented an apartment to plan the attack and in the basement of which her co-conspirators had parked the VW bus. The young Dutch people also had a VW bus. They too parked it in the basement garage. The next morning, they found the windscreen and all four tyres slashed.

The search intensified, with some near-successes, and a disaster or two. On autobahns in North-Rhine-Westphalia, traffic was watched by patrol cars from which the registration of the passing vehicles could be fed directly into the Wiesbaden computer; camping sites were searched; estate agents were told to report newly leased flats.

A second commando apartment was found in Cologne in a Y-shaped building, 43-storeys high, which contained 554 apartments. In the basement garage, there was an Alfa-Romeo Julia 1600, registration K-XY 847. Enquiries from the plate-makers showed that the same number had been printed eight times. Papers in the car showed that the owner was called 'Konrad Binder'. Binder was a pseudonym for the terrorist, Rolf Heissler, who had once belonged to an extremist group called the Tupamaros Munich and was wanted for complicity in the murders of Buback and Ponto. The whole block was raided. Three hundred officials took part in the raid, most of them in civil dress. On the 26th floor was found the hiding place of Adelheid Schulz, wanted for complicity in the Buback murder. The police searched the rest of the building, forcing their way into every flat. If the occupant was not in, they left behind a note, apologizing for their action and asking for understanding and co-operation. They found nothing.

In Utrecht, the Dutch police muffed a chance of a capture. Checking out a car rental company, police discovered that a certain 'Astrid Winter' from Hamburg, who wanted to extend the hiring time of the car, had false papers. When she came into the building again, accompanied by a young man, the police were ready. But at the shout 'Police! Hands up!' the young man immediately pulled a gun and opened fire. One policeman was killed instantly. The man was overpowered: he was one of the assumed kidnappers, Knut Folkerts. The woman escaped. The woman was identified from fingerprints as one of the wanted terrorists – Brigitte Mohnhaupt.

The police were ready to adopt unorthodox methods. When a woman from Bavaria called up to say that she had had the same dream three days running which indicated Schleyer was being held in a baroque or rococo house in Cologne whose windows were hung with newspapers, detectives were immediately detailed to find the house. They were unsuccessful. Another time, a diviner went over a map of Cologne with his branch. When it twitched, he said, 'Schleyer is hidden here.' Again, nothing was found. Two members of the Anti-Terrorist Department, accompanied by the psychologist, Salewski, even went to see the Dutch clairvoyant, Gerard Croiset, in Utrecht, who indicated Schleyer's hiding place as being a particular area, Meschenich, on the outskirts of Cologne; but he could not be exact. He had already read so much about the case, he said, that his clairvoyant powers were blurred.

Meanwhile Schleyer's kidnappers, who by now had extended the deadline to September 14, had put forward a new suggestion through Payot. The Siegfried Hausner Commando would forego the peak time television announcement after the release of the eleven prisoners, if instead an announcement was made two hours after the end of all the programmes on September 14.

The suggestion set in motion a novel investigation which led to a significant break-through – and also provided one of the most extraordinary vindications of paranormal abilities.

On the night of September 14–15, a VW van with detection antennae drove around the Cologne area indicated by Croiset, between 1.00 a.m. and 3.00 a.m., trying to detect televisions that were still turned on. They found six TVs which were still turned on. They were all false alarms except one, which was traced to a huge apartment building. It was indeed still in the area that Croiset had indicated, but there were 1,750 flats in the block and the detection apparatus could not identify which one the television was in.

But in the basement, the police found a Mercedes, registration BM-A 812. A swift check showed that the registration was false. The ignition keys were found in the exhaust. For eight days, the police kept watch; then they concluded that the car had been abandoned. The car was opened and searched. Inside was a veritable treasure trove. Under a mat they found the case of a sub-machine gun bullet. Laboratory tests showed that the shell had been used in one of the weapons fired during the Schleyer raid. In addition, in the boot lay a lapis lazuli cuff-link. It was flown immediately to Stuttgart and identified by Waltrude Schleyer as one of her husband's. And finally, a hole had been cut between the boot and the rear of the back seat – clearly an air hole that had been used during the transportation of Schleyer.

Now came the search of the apartment block itself. This had not been done before in case the kidnappers were in there and killed Schleyer. But nothing was found (at least nothing to do with Schleyer: in one of the flats, police found the corpse of a six-month-old child who had been dead for two weeks; and in another, a 'lesbian apartment' – at least that was what the neighbours called it – there were, of all things, fourteen dogs).

The police established that the Mercedes had been bought by Willy Peter Stoll in Bensberg. Stoll had given the name, Martin Klas. He had driven to the dealer in a taxi, carrying the money in plastic bags.

On the night of September 24–25 came another near miss. From a telephone box near Cologne Cathedral, a woman called up Denis Payot in Geneva. It was picked up by a tap and a patrol car was dispatched immediately. The telephone tappers made a faulty connection. One of the men said 'Hey, Karl, I think they're on again.' The woman hung up directly. Twenty-five seconds later the patrol car arrived at the telephone box. It was empty. Later a voice print showed that the caller had probably been the terrorist, Adelheid Schulz.

So gradually, piece by piece, the police were able to put together a picture of the crime. Their work was made somewhat easier by the fact that the kidnappers were great ones for sending letters. Up until October 13 – the date on which the Schleyer drama escalated with the hijacking of the Lufthansa jet – 47 letters had been received. They comprised copies of three main texts. The police established that the kidnappers had three photocopying machines and six typewriters and – because the letters had been despatched in three separate batches – they indicated that the hostage had been held in three different places. The police assumed that the pauses between the batches meant a change of hiding-place. They were also able to reconstruct the origins of the polaroid film and the video-tapes. The tape of Schleyer was made with the same machine as the one that recorded Schmidt's *Gartenfest* for which Christoph Wackernagel had spoken the commentary.

Soon police were able to list those probably involved: the Mercedes which blocked Schleyer's convoy was driven either by Silke Maier-Witt or Angelika Speitel; and the killers were almost certainly Willy Peter Stoll, Christian Klar, Rolf Clemens Wagner, Rolf Heissler and Friederike Krabbe. The

VW bus was probably chauffeured by Knut Folkerts.

The terrorists had laid many false clues. On the first video-tape there was a Swiss milk bottle. Soon afterwards, the police found a VW bus near Lörrach on the Swiss border which contained one of Schleyer's ties and a leather key-case with keys. The investigators guessed that this was a decoy to switch their attentions to southern Germany. Even the clicking of a woman's high-heeled shoes on stairs was, it was thought, an attempt by the terrorists to give the impression that Schleyer was being held aboard ship.

ON THE INSIDE

At 3.00 a.m. on the 6th, nine and a half hours after the kidnapping, the psychologist Wolfgang Salewski, of Munich arrived in the Bonn branch of the Criminal Office. Salewski, who had been responsible for a Lufthansa informational film on how to deal with hijackers, was much in demand as an adviser (his fee: 2,000 marks a day). After the Munich debacle of 1972, Salewski had devised a technique for dealing with kidnappers.

Salewski's theory was straightforward enough. It was based on the simple assumption that as long as there was communication with the kidnappers, nothing bad would happen. Tricks and threats were out; instead of them, Salewski said: 'You have to have a bit of understanding for their point of view. Don't look at them *just* as criminals. Look at the situation that they're in. What you must do is create a situation so stable that the terrorists don't crack up. That does not mean to say that you give in to everything that they ask. On the contrary, that would make them suspicious. They must have the feeling that things are moving in their direction. If the two sides keep talking, some sort of a relationship can develop. That way, you stand a chance of exercising some control and thus give the hostage a chance of life.'

Would practice conform with theory? Would the terrorists co-operate and, in particular, how would the victim react?

To get an answer to this last question Schmidt called Schleyer's eldest son, Hanns-Eberhard, one week after the kidnapping. The call lasted one and a half hours.

Schmidt wanted to know about Schleyer's health and personality. For 62, he was healthy, replied Hanns-Eberhard, calmly, precisely, professionally. His father had come back from holiday a few weeks earlier. He did not need any special medicine regularly. 'He can survive through 14 days of captivity okay." Fourteen days! That was twice the length of Lorenz's captivity in 1975 and it was as much as the family thought he would have to endure.

Hanns-Eberhard promised that the family would behave as his father apparently wished – to follow the government's lead and not disrupt the negotiations by their own actions.

Gradually, the government and police began to build up a portrait of Schleyer's personality. They were relieved to find he was not as uncompromising as he seemed on television.

Schleyer, his acquaintances and family agreed, was a friendly character. They had anecdotes to prove it. Marcisz, his driver, had asked Schleyer to call him by his christian name and Schleyer had said that he should do the same. Before Schleyer moved to Raschdorffstrasse he used to live in Domstrasse, just by the centre of Cologne. It was a shady quarter, full of petty criminals and pimps. When they learned who their new neighbour was, some of them rang on the door bell and introduced themselves. Schleyer went out for a beer with them. Jörg remembered: 'They used to call my father "Ham" [*H*anns-*M*artin].' When his wife and police said that he should move for security reasons, he refused. 'I am quite happy where I am,' he said, 'nothing can happen to me here. I am right in the middle of it. If anyone else tries to muscle in, there will be real trouble from the others.' He moved only because he began to come to Cologne more and more frequently and the old flat was too small. There seemed some hope, then, that Schleyer would not antagonize his captors.

On September 8, Schleyer wrote to his son, Hans-Eberhard: 'Greetings to you all. You are much in my thoughts. My health is good but I don't have enough information about events and have to rely on my captors so I find it hard to assess the significance of the following thoughts. . . . If the demands are not met and I am killed, the kidnappers will seize another hostage, so it is worth weighing the consequences of my death . . . I am certainly not going to break down, so you can all keep happy and cheerful. I have been in tough situations before and come through all right. Lots of kisses to Mummy and to you all. I will see you soon I hope. Daddy.'

Among the crisis staff, the decision was clear from the start: there would be no giving in. Schmidt and Kohl agreed privately on a hard line. It was all very different to the circumstances surrounding the kidnapping of Peter Lorenz in 1975. Then, both Kohl and the S.P.D. mayor of West Berlin, Klaus Schütz, had been all for an exchange, as had Franz Josef Strauss. Now nobody spoke up strongly for an exchange.

There were only two vague, insignificant and temporary cracks in this unity. C.D.U. Minister-President, Hans Filbinger, wondered briefly whether it would not be worth while exchanging two rather than all eleven terrorists, a suggestion that aroused only amazement and no interest. And Franz Josef Strauss rhetorically asked what an exchange would mean, although he never came out strongly for such a course.

Hanns-Eberhard, however, was understandably driven by personal loyalties as well as national ones. He wanted an exchange, and put his case through a colleague, Peter Mailänder, in the *Stuttgarter Zeitung*, under the headline 'A Decision Necessary for Life'. The article argued that the Basic Law – West Germany's Constitution – established the sanctity of human life as an overriding principle and that there was no alternative but to fulfil the demands of the terrorists.

Hanns-Eberhard did not want to leave it simply as an appeal in a newspaper. He wanted the Constitutional Court to force his rights on the government and so secure the release of the hostage. But legally, his argument was a little weak. A counter-argument would run as follows: The Basic Law establishes a duty to protect not only individual citizens, but also the whole community. A full awareness of this duty demands that the State be in a position to react to circumstances as they arise. The State cannot protect the individual if its action thereby threatens others – as it would if killers were released to kill again. The law cannot specify a single response; if it did, terrorists would know what to plan for, and terrorism would be aided, not curbed.

Later, Hanns-Eberhard tried to buy his father's freedom. In compliance with one of the terrorists' demands, he packed up 15 million U.S. dollars in three Samsonite bags. The money, provided by the Federal Bank, was in marks, Dutch gilders, Swiss francs and U.S. dollars. He planned to meet the kidnappers in the Frankfurt Intercontinental. They were to approach him with a code-phrase, in English: 'Let us save your father.' He was to reply, also in English: 'We shall save my father.'

The government supported the deal. But DPA, the German Press Agency, leaked the news, with the result that 100 journalists and two television teams arrived to cover the transaction. Not surprisingly, it did not take place.

Next Hanns-Eberhard told the kidnappers that he was ready to fly anywhere in the world to hand over the money. They suggested a meeting in Paris. When Hanns-Eberhard wanted to know how he was supposed to carry the money – the three cases weighed some 250 pounds – the reply came, 'Oh, there are lots of police near you. It would be good training for them to take the cases to the airport. The airline can handle them from there.' But then the terrorists backed out because the government was not ready to release the prisoners. There were no further contacts.

Tragically, as the days passed without any new leads, the Schleyer family became increasingly demoralized and isolated. They began to argue. Arndt demanded that the family impose some public pressure on the government. Hanns-Eberhard countered by saying that there was more than the government involved – pressure would have to involve the whole crisis staff, with representatives of all parties, and the police. And without public support, the family could not hope for any success. But there was nothing to tell the media. They tried, nevertheless. One week after the abduction, Waltrude Schleyer made an appeal through *Bild Zeitung*: 'Exchange him!' The next day, there were countless calls criticizing her action. Almost unanimously, the callers told the family to hold back: if the terrorists were released, more people would be killed. The family retreated into its shell.

On September 9, Hanns Martin Schleyer said in a handwritten letter to a friend, Eberhard von Brauchitsch: 'The demand for a go-between [i.e. Payot] is utter nonsense because my kidnappers will not reveal themselves or our "holiday-place" to a go-between, so that a three-way contact is impossible. The uncertainty of my situation is terrible, of course. If Bonn is going to reject the demands they should do it soon, although anyone – as in time of war – would want to survive.'

The letter caused consternation among the police, not because it contained the first signs of panic – that would not alter the hard-line decision – but because it looked as if the message might contain some hidden information. The phrase, 'three-way contact', was written strangely, in two words, without a hyphen (*Dreiecks Kontakt*). Was Schleyer trying to indicate that his hiding-place lay in the Aachen area, where three countries – Holland, Belgium and Germany – met; or in a corner of the south where Switzerland, Germany and France came together? Then there was the question of the 'holiday-place', in quotes and in close proximity to the German word '*dass*', its *-ss*' written, not as Schleyer usually wrote it, with the German letter (-ß), but in the English fashion with two s's. Could this be a reference to his time with the S.S.?

The police, helped by Hanns-Eberhard, began to ask all of Schleyer's old S.S. friends about any communal holiday places. But there was more guessing than decoding. A massive search began on both sides of the Franco-German border. It is still going on. No one yet knows if the whole thing was a red herring.

Only one thing emerged. When the kidnappers realized that the search was escalating, they demanded yet again, through Denis Payot, that the manhunt be called off. The police replied: 'We are not looking for the kidnappers; we are looking for the murderers of Siegfried Buback and Jürgen Ponto.' The 'Siegfried Hausner Commando' said that they wanted the manhunt for *all* R.A.F. people called off. This was their first acknowledgement that both murders were done by the R.A.F. Until then, the only link had been a statement by Susanne Albrecht that she had shot Ponto.

On September 12, Schleyer sent a tape to Helmut Kohl. 'The situation in which I find myself is politically incomprehensible. I have never made a fuss about my life. ... but what you are imposing on me is senseless torture. I am not prepared to leave this life silently just to cover up the mistakes of the government and of the political parties and the inadequacies of your much-vaunted Criminal Office bosses.'

At a meeting of the crisis staff, Strauss asked Salewski how a hostage in the power 'of these mad people' could so insult the police and the government. 'That's fear,' replied Salewski, 'not Schleyer's fear, but that of the terrorists who told him to say what he said. When I am frightened, I have to build up a picture of an enemy that I can strike out at.' To which Hanns Eberhard added that the expression 'much-vaunted bosses' was not in his father's style. 'I know he has a lot of endurance,' he added, optimistically, 'he'll take the whole thing as a personal challenge, which is how he used to respond to difficulties in business or union politics.'

On September 14, another video-tape of Schleyer was handed over to the French news agency, A.F.P., in the Hotel Bristol in Bonn. His messages were becoming increasingly strident: 'I have repeatedly said that I will support any decision reached by the government, whatever it may be. But the activities of the police in my opinion are merely tricks to win time ... I cannot imagine that those who are politically responsible intend to create the official impression that the demands are to be fulfilled, when in reality they plan no such thing ... I am greatly concerned that the authorities want my death to conceal their mistakes.'

Schleyer was right: the police were using tricks to gain time. But the fact that the gang sent such accusations showed that the tactics were working. The Criminal Office diary for the 14th read in part: 'The terrorists seem stable in their behaviour. As we pursue the strategy of going along with the demands step by step we have to guarantee the continuation of that stability.' There were many indications that the situation had become less tense. In telephone calls the kidnappers often ended with the words: 'Many thanks, and have a good evening,' without any apparent sarcasm. In one phone call with Hanns-Eberhard's wife, who was tense and angry, they said soothingly that they hoped everything would work out and that it would be possible to 'arrange matters of common interest.' Salewski commented jokingly, 'they will sign the next letter "Yours sincerely".'

In accordance with the official tactics to undertake activities seemingly in accord with the R.A.F. demands, the prisoners were asked about their ultimate destinations. Three of them, Hanna Krabbe, Karl-Heinz Dellwo and Bernd Rösner, did not even fill out their questionnaires. Andreas Baader named five destinations: Algeria, Libya, Vietnam, Iraq and South Yemen. Raspe put the same names and added: Angola, Mozambique, Guinea-Bissau, and Ethiopia (additions that seem to indicate that he had spoken to Baader, despite the ban on contacts). The others said that they just wanted to be flown out without naming a destination.

The number of destinations gave the government and the police a new reason to delay. The police noted for the record: 'Start talks with the countries concerned, make clear that departure without having a place to go is nonsensical ... as long as the government and the police seem to be preparing to grant the demands, there is no actual danger to Schleyer. Continue negotiations according to the approved strategy.'

Hans-Jürgen Wischnewski, Minister of State in the Chancellor's Office, was given the task of travelling abroad in this half-practical, half-spurious display of activity. He was a good choice: his wide experience in Arab affairs had earned him the nickname 'Ben Wisch'. First he went to Algeria. The Algerians were in a somewhat delicate situation. They were due to have a meeting with the Confederation of German Industry, whose leader was to have been Hanns-Martin Schleyer. Government officials told Wischnewski: 'We don't want to have anything to do with the kidnappers.' They did not want to be denounced as the friend of terrorists. Still, they did not want to be responsible for Schleyer's death, and would help if the German government asked them to for 'humanitarian reasons'.

In Tripoli, Wischnewski's next stop, he came up against outright hostility. Libya's President Ghadafi told Wischnewski that he was very annoyed at always being described in German newspapers as the financier of international terrorism.

Negotiations in Aden, the next stop, were somewhat delicate. South Yemen had, in 1975, taken the five kidnappers of Peter Lorenz. They had done so on condition that Bonn would make an extradition request for them two weeks later. The Yemenis had therefore put the five Germans under house arrest immediately after their arrival. Bonn never did make its request for extradition: Berlin vetoed the move for fear of terrorist reprisals. Now the Yemenis said they would never take any German terrorists again.

In Iraq, Wischnewski was spared an outright No. The government said it would tell him later of its decision. It never did.

Wischnewski was unable to land in Hanoi because it was being rebuilt and the military base there could not take large jets. He had to land in Saigon, where he stayed in the old Intercontinental Hotel. He met an official of the Vietnamese government, who was very disappointed that Wischnewski only wanted to talk about prisoners. He thought the German had flown in to talk about aid. The government was not interested in terrorists: 'You could have saved yourself the long flight,' Wischnewski was told.

So the strategy of establishing that no country would take the R.A.F. prisoners had almost worked out.

Back in Bonn, officials in the Interior Ministry, the Justice Ministry and the Chancellor's Office discussed new and exotic scenarios, only to discard them again. Could 'psycho-drugs' be used to get Baader and Raspe to reveal their connections with the kidnappers? Or to get the terrorist Knut Folkerts – who had meanwhile been arrested in Holland – to reveal Schleyer's hiding place? Or perhaps the prisoners could be flown out and then secret services agents – the C.I.A. or the Israelis – could get on their trail and arrest them again or liquidate them?

The most extraordinary suggestion was that somewhere in the Middle East a cardboard airport could be put up which would fool the terrorists that they had arrived at one of their destinations. Israel even offered help and a place to construct the stage-set. As soon as the terrorists sent word to release Schleyer, the whole lot could be recaptured and flown back again.

But nothing practical emerged. How much longer could the affair drag on? The thought obviously obsessed both the kidnappers and Schleyer. On a last video-tape, sent via Payot, Schleyer said: 'I ask myself, what has to happen to make Bonn make up its mind? I have now been in terrorist hands for five and a half weeks, and I am here because I worked for years for this country and for its free and democratic system. Sometimes it strikes me what a mockery all this activity has been.' Daily the fear grew that the kidnappers might undertake a second action to impose additional pressure on Schmidt.

On October 13, it happened. Four Palestinians hijacked a Lufthansa jet.

4. THE TAKING OF LH181

THE HIJACKING

On October 6, 1977, towards 11.00 p.m., a young man with black hair appeared in the lobby of the Saratoga Hotel in Palma, Majorca. The 100-bed, three-star hotel lay on Jaime III Street and the Passeo Generalissimo Franco, where the large travel agencies have their headquarters. The man carried a bag and a large red suitcase. Speaking English with a strong accent, he asked for a single room. He had not booked. The head porter, Señor Cardona, apologized: 'I'm sorry; I can't do anything for you,' he said, 'we're booked up. But wait a minute; perhaps I can offer you something, just for tonight. A room with four beds? It'll be more expensive, of course. . . .'

The young man said that did not matter. The main thing was that he should have a bed. Perhaps tomorrow a single room would fall free. He filled out his resident's card. He gave his name as Ali Hyderi, an Iranian. He received the registration number 146380.

The next morning Hyderi again asked for a single room. Again, there were none free. This time he got a double room. Hyderi asked a little uncertainly: 'Isn't there anything else free? I'm expecting somebody this evening, about midnight.'

'Well, you've got a double room,' the porter suggested, 'perhaps your friend can sleep in your room tonight?'

'It's a woman.'

The porter shrugged: 'That's your affair.'

'Well, I'll manage,' replied Hyderi.

Towards midnight, a young woman with strikingly beautiful eyes arrived at the hotel. She carried a bag and a light-blue make-up case. Hyderi was waiting for her in the lobby. They greeted each other like old, but not particularly close acquaintances.

The girl also had an Iranian passport. She registered as Soraya Ansari, born in 1954 in Teheran. The couple went up to Hyderi's room.

The next day, the 8th, a group of tourists arrived at the hotel. They had a block booking; the couple could not stay any longer. They checked into a double room in the neighbouring three-star hotel, Jaime III.

The next morning they ordered breakfast in their room. When the maid knocked at 10.00 a.m. she found the room empty. She put down the tray on the table. From noises in the bathroom, the maid concluded that the two were having a bath together.

In the same hotel there was another couple with Iranian passports. They had been there for several days. They went by the names of Riza Abbasi and Shanaz Gholoun. The receptionist noticed them because they were both extraordinarily good-looking.

The 'Iranians' were not, of course, really Iranians. They came from Israel and Lebanon. Riza Abbasi, 23, was born in Beirut as Wabil Harb, the son of a well-to-do Lebanese. In the Lebanese Civil War he fought on the Moslem side and became fanatically pro-Palestinian. His room-mate, Shanaz Gholoun, was Hind Alameh, 22, a Lebanese Christian who fell in love with a Palestinian and became a radical follower of the Palestinian Left. Soraya Ansari was Suhaila Sayeh, 22, born in Israel, whose Christian parents emigrated to Kuwait, taking her with them. She studied English literature in Baghdad. During the Lebanese Civil War, she survived the Christians' massacre of Palestinians in the Tel Zataar refugee camp.

Ali Hyderi, 23, was born in the Palestinian refugee camp of Burj el-Brajneh on the edge of Beirut. His real name was Zohair Yousif Akache. His Palestinian parents had fled from the Israelis in 1948. He was the leader of the small team, and a certain amount is known about him.

Akache was one of the few young people who managed to work his way out of the horrors of the camp where he was born. He did so by hard work, intelligence, and political fanaticism. As a teenager, he attached himself to George Habash's Popular Front for the Liberation of Palestine (P.F.L.P.). On January 2, 1973, he became a student at the independent Chelsea College of Aeronautical and Automobile Engineering, then actually based in Chelsea and now in Shoreham, Sussex. He learnt to fly in a Cessna. Two years later, he qualified.

Akache lived in squalor. In his £5.00-per-week room (at 38 Longridge Road, Earls Court) he papered the filthy walls with Palestinian posters. In the blank spaces, he scrawled Palestinian slogans in felt-tipped pen. His acquaintances from those days remember him as a lonely and intelligent character, companionable as long as no one mentioned the Palestinian situation. He once struck out with a knife at a countryman who expressed the opinion that the Palestinian problem should be solved politically by the Americans and the Russians. Sometimes he would go drinking in the King's Head, near Earls Court station, returning home shouting Palestinian slogans and ready to make trouble with neighbours or police.

He first came to the attention of Scotland Yard in December 1974 at a relatively peaceful pro-Palestinian demonstration in Trafalgar Square. He attacked police, was arrested, and was identified as a P.F.L.P. activist. But then, instead of being extradited, was allowed to go on with his studies.

It was about this time that Akache got to know a Yugoslavian girl, Branka Ninkovic. Later, after the hijacking, she described Akache as a 'tender, sensitive and romantic man.' Branka Ninkovic was in London working and learning English. She lived with Akache for six months in his small room in Earls Court. The couple were surrounded by Palestinian flags, Palestinian posters, pictures of Arafat, Habash, Nasser, Che Guevara and Palestinian war heroes, yet she only saw anything of his extremism when he went to give speeches at Hyde Park Corner on Saturdays. He had nothing against his Jewish landlord. As he explained: 'Why should I have anything against Jews in England, Spain or Yugoslavia?' he said to her, 'I only hate the Jews who have robbed me of my homeland.'

Branka provided odd little details about Akache. He kept two tame mice in his room, whom he called Jim and Jack. When Jim died and Branka tossed the tiny corpse into the dustbin, Akache became quite angry; he wrapped the mouse in a piece of paper and laid it out in the grass in Hyde Park. He was vain: he liked dark colours and hated tight trousers because 'he didn't want to look like one of those English queers.' He had a fad for cleanliness and often had two baths a day. He changed his bed-linen every other day and became angry if Branka used his handkerchief.

Branka found she was pregnant shortly after she got to know him. She was nervous that the child was that of an Englishman, with whom she had broken soon after meeting Zohair. She wanted to have an abortion, but Akache insisted that they should get married. Branka, nervous of having a fair child obviously not his, flew back to Yugoslavia. The child was indeed fair. He wrote to her tenderly several times, believing the child to be his. She never told him the truth.

In late 1975, there was another demonstration in Hyde Park. Once again, Akache got into a fight with police. This time he was given six months in Pentonville. While there he went on hunger strike. After two weeks he was admitted to St. Olave's Hospital in Southwark. On March 26, 1976, two Special Branch officers took him to Heathrow and put him on a plane to Beirut.

In early 1977, he was back in London. He had a Kuwaiti passport in the name of Achmed Badr. He stayed for a month in an Indian haunt, the Queen's Hotel, Bayswater. Then he vanished. On March 23, he landed at Heathrow again, and passed through Passport Control as a Kuwaiti called Adel Hassan.

On April 5, he booked into the Robert House Hotel, Westbourne Street. From his room on the third floor he could see the Royal Lancaster Hotel, in which the former Prime Minister of North Yemen, Abdullah al-Hajari, lived with his wife, Fatima. The ex-Premier had supposedly been responsible for the death of left-wing opponents.

On the morning of April 10, Easter Sunday, the Yemeni couple came out of the hotel and began to get into a Mercedes with a member of their Embassy. Akache was waiting behind the car. He went slowly round to the right-hand front doot. The engine was already running. Akache opened the door with his left hand. In his right he held a pistol with a silencer. He shot the former Premier in the head, then fired at his wife and the diplomat. All three died. Akache took another couple of steps, turned round, shot twice through the windscreen, and then vanished among the crowds of pedestrians.

Scotland Yard had been watching the Palestinian, but the police were not immediately able to identify the attacker as Akache, who slipped out via Heathrow on an Iraqi Airlines flight for Baghdad that same afternoon.

From Baghdad he went to a Palestinian camp 50 miles outside the town. There, under the leadership of Dr. Wadi Haddad, the 'Special Operations Division' of the P.F.L.P. were in training. Six months later, as the German government stalled over the demands made by Schleyer's kidnappers, four of the best on the training course – Wabil Harb, Hind Alameh, Suhaila Sayeh and Zohair Youssif Akache – were chosen to fly to Majorca for the next 'special operation', the hijacking of a Lufthansa plane.

Almost daily Wabil Harb had been into a number of travel agencies. On October 4, for instance, he went into the Euroclub Agency on Jaime III Street. He said that he wanted to fly Lufthansa from Palma to Frankfurt sometime in the next few days. 'I have to fly Lufthansa,' he said insistently, 'and it must be during the week, not at a weekend.'

The Euroclub employee told him there was only one possible flight – Lufthansa 181 on Thursday, October 6.

Harb said he did not know whether that would work. He would have to have a talk with his friends.

The next day, he returned to Euroclub. The Thursday flight would be a little early for him. Wasn't there anything later?

Well, that was difficult with Lufthansa, the man said, because it was so booked up. Couldn't he fly Iberia?

The young man again insisted: 'No, it has to be Lufthansa.'

On October 6, Harb was back again. The Euroclub man made him a suggestion: 'If you really must fly Lufthansa, why don't you fly Iberia to Barcelona? A Lufthansa flight leaves there every day for Frankfurt.'

Harb put himself down for the connecting flight on October 10. The Euroclub man called up to confirm the flight, then announced in embarrassment, 'I'm sorry; the Lufthansa flight is booked up.'

Harb left and returned very early the next day. This time, he asked whether he could fly direct to Frankfurt on the following Thursday, the 13th. Yes, he could. He booked for two people and bought two first-class tickets. He paid cash in dollars.

The same day at 11.30 a.m. Akache went to another travel agency, Viajes Iberia S.A., on the Passeo Generalissimo Franco and ordered two tickets to Frankfurt on the 13th, also on Lufthansa 181. Akache paid for two economy tickets in dollars.

The two couples with Iranian passports changed hotels once more.

Akache and Suhaila Sayeh went to the expensive Bellver, a lush, 14-storey hotel with marble fronted pillars in the hall and imitation English furniture in its 400 rooms. The girl was so striking that she was immediately noticed. The couple behaved like average tourists. Only once – on the evening of October 12 – did they attract attention. They came into the lobby arm-in-arm. Suhaila had a large bunch of roses in her arms. She looked extremely happy. A few tipsy guests congratulated them and wanted to know whether they were celebrating their engagement or their wedding. The two were apparently irritated. They made no reply and went straight up to their room.

Wabil Harb and Hind Alameh went to the Costa Azul on October 10. The next evening they were visited by the other two. Suhaila went to the porter and asked him to reserve four places for a flamenco show in the Torre del Oro. The four of them went out for the evening and came back late that night.

The next evening, the 12th, they packed – a few red T-shirts with a portrait of Che Guevara bought in a Palma boutique; a Russian Makarow pistol; a Hungarian Tokarev pistol; a considerable amount of 9-mm ammunition; six home-made hand-grenades, and some 60 pounds of plasticine-like explosive. The T-shirts were put into a travelling bag. The other objects were stowed into a large, specially prepared radio, spray cans, the blue make-up case and the large red suitcase.

That evening, the 12th, Lufthansa stewardess Gabriele Dillmann – Gaby as she was known – was in the kitchen of her Frankfurt apartment. She was trying to cook *Züricher Geschnetzeltes* – a finely-chopped meat dish from Switzerland – for the first time. Her friend, Rüdeger von Lutzau, a Lufthansa co-pilot, was helping her. He had asked her to cook something totally new. It was a success. After the meal, the two of them sat down to watch some television.

The next day, Gaby was scheduled on a one-day trip to Palma in a Boeing 737. Then she was to be on standby in Frankfurt.

'Let's hope you won't have to go out tomorrow evening again' said Rüdeger, who was due to have a housewarming the following evening at his new flat. It was going to be a stag party. Gaby was going to make a potato salad.

'I'd better do the washing up,' she said, then added: 'No, I'll leave it until tomorrow when you are having fun with your pals.'

They went to bed and, as he often did after they had made love, Rüdeger talked about marriage. 'Well,' he joked, 'don't you count *that* as a proposal of marriage?' Gaby laughed, as usual: 'Certainly not. If you want to propose to me, you'll have to do it properly. In a suit, kneeling and holding a bunch of flowers.'

Gaby, at 23, had already been with Lufthansa for three years. She had actually wanted to be a vet, but she had not made the grade academically. She had known Rüdeger since June and she too had considered marriage, but thought that one should wait a year or so, to make sure.

The next morning, October 13, Gaby and Rüdeger left for the airport shortly before 8.00 a.m. The day began well: they found a space in the basement garage immediately. Rüdeger walked Gaby up to the briefing room and said: 'Tomorrow afternoon, if they put you on standby, give me a call, and I'll come by for a cup of coffee.' He wrote down his office telephone number – he was acting as a coordinator for flight staff between his own flights – gave her a kiss and left.

At the briefing, Gaby introduced herself to the other members of the crew. She only knew one of them, Captain Jürgen Schumann, a replacement for the original pilot, who was fog-bound in Hamburg. She had already done two five-day tours with him. Gaby found most of the pilots a little conceited, but with Schumann, a former Starfighter pilot, she had established an immediate rapport. It turned out that they had been to the same school.

There was one member of the crew missing: the co-pilot, Jürgen Vietor.

Vietor had woken up early that morning in the terraced house where he and his wife, Renate, lived in Bensheim, 30 miles south of Frankfurt. He switched on the radio to listen to the weather forecast, which immediately threw him into a bad mood: there was fog everywhere and he was on standby. If it remained foggy, he knew he could count on at least one 737 crew being off schedule, which would mean that he would have to fly.

He guessed right. At 7.00 a.m. the phone rang and a cheery Lufthansa voice announced: 'Herr Vietor, congratulations! You've won a free return flight to Palma.' Departure time was 8.55 a.m.

To make the briefing, half an hour before the take off time, he should have left already. His case was already packed. But for some reason he had misheard the flight time. He drank a cup of coffee, read a paper, and day-dreamed. Renate, a teacher, left for work. Soon after 8.00 a.m. the phone went again: 'For heaven's sake man, didn't you know that there was a briefing?' Vietor made his hurried and embarrassed apologies and promised, 'I'll be at the plane in half an hour.'

It was the first time in four years that he had ever been late. Punctuality, conscientiousness, regularity were his prime virtues. His career had been varied, if not dramatic – an apprentice in electrical engineering; a radio operator in the army; naval officer candidate; flying school; an officer in the Fleet Air-arm with 3,000 hours of flying experience; and finally, in 1973, to Lufthansa. He had been a 737 co-pilot since 1974. He had few ambitions. He thought he could see his future fairly clearly. He reckoned that he would not become a captain before his mid-40's – the times of rapid promotion in Lufthansa were over and most of the captains were relatively young. On this steady foundation, he and Renate were saving for a house.

Vietor had more experience with 737's than most captains, who often started on other planes. Although the 737 was not particularly comfortable, he was fond of it, as were many of the staff, who had given it endearing, if derogatory nicknames – Bobby, Piglet, Fatty.

The 737 intended for the Palma flight was called 'Landshut'. All Lufthansa's 737's – short-haul 'city-jets' – carry German place-names. The Landshut, named after a town 40 miles north-east of Munich, had not originally been intended for this flight. It had brought some freight in from Geneva and was to have flown on to Hamburg, but because of the fog, planes were scarce in Frankfurt and it was switched to the Palma run.

Vietor raced to the airport in his Peugeot 304, covering the 25 miles at speeds up to 100 m.p.h. The crew was already on board when he arrived. He excused himself and introduced himself to the captain, Schumann, to the Austrian chief stewardess, Hannelore Piegler, and the two other stewardesses, a Norwegian, Anna-Maria Staringer, and to Gaby Dillmann.

Vietor knew none of them, which was a little unusual after four years of flying in a 'Bobby'. He had never even seen the captain before, for Schumann had been on 737's only a few months.

The Landshut closed its doors punctually at 8.55. But then there was a delay – eight planes were awaiting take-off. Vietor, still a bit out of breath after his sprint through the airport buildings, made the flight control check. Schumann was going to fly the first leg – it was usual on one-day trips for the captain to fly out and the co-pilot to fly back.

Gaby Dillmann, working in the economy section, was normally a slow starter. This morning however she was in a good mood. She liked one-day tours, especially when Rüdeger was not flying and she could see him again the same evening. And she liked tourist flights. She would rather have excited pensioners and young people on holiday than darksuited business people who never said 'Thank you.' She would rather have people like the nervous old grandmother who needed reassurance and a cup of coffee and who finally relaxed and said: 'Oh, there's coffee, is there? Thank you, *Fräulein.*'

On Majorca itself at about this time, a number of the passengers were preparing for their departure on LH181 at 11.00 a.m.

A 26-year-old teacher, Hartwig Faby, from Stade, near Hamburg, had been staying with a friend, Rhett Waida, who happened to have a house on the island. Hartwig Faby was not all that keen on beaches and sun. He had accompanied his friend, and his three-year-old son Steffen because he had never flown before and wanted to see an aeroplane from the inside.

The two of them had to return that Thursday, because the next day was Herr Waida's birthday and they were due to celebrate together with their wives. Towards 11.00 a.m. the two men, along with Steffen, arrived at Palma airport.

In another house not far away a local business man, Hans Hasse Heyn, began to pack a few things into a bag. He paused to take a slug on whisky. Heyn often began the day with whisky. Once a counter-intelligence officer in Hitler's Wehrmacht, he had escaped from the French at the end of the war and remained in Spain. He had tried many occupations. Now, at 67, he made a good living in Majorca from the tourists and as a boxing promoter. He was going to do some business in Frankfurt and in Düsseldorf.

Heyn believed that the secret of his success lay in his intuition. At the airport he told his driver and his private secretary, Don Vicente Gonzáles: 'Have all my papers photocopied – the deeds of the house, working papers, the lot – in case anything happens to me.' Then he loaded up with several bottles of spirit and went into the bar to have a beer.

Lilo Cramer – her real name has been altered at her own request – was due in Munich the next weekend to meet a friend, much to the annoyance of her husband, David, who wanted her to stay until the following week. He had become quite angry: 'You're only going to play rummy the whole time!'

Lilo Cramer, 56, was born a Jew in Krakow, Poland. Her father died in Buchenwald, her sister and two children in Auschwitz. Her brother was taken away by the Gestapo and never heard of again. Lilo herself had been hidden by friends during the war. She had never lost her fear of anti-Semitism. She was afraid of people who looked Arabic. The previous week, she and her husband had been having supper on the terrace of the Victoria Hotel in Palma when they had noticed a couple that looked middle-eastern. Half joking, half seriously, Lilo said to her husband: 'Look how well they live on their holdups!'

On the way to the airport, Lilo and David were still angry with each other. They did not exchange a word. Usually, David accompanied his wife to the barrier and then watched from the observation platform until the plane took off. Now, for the first time since they were married, he left her in the foyer without so much as a kiss.

In the departure lounge, Lilo Cramer thought for a moment that she spotted the 'orientals' she had seen in the restaurant, but she dismissed the thought immediately. She tended to have gloomy premonitions; her husband and friends laughed at her for it. Still, 'just in case,' she bought some food, some biscuits and a stick of English rock.

The last passengers at the check-in were a group of extremely attractive German girls who were clearly the worse for a hard night. They were finalists of beauty contests put on by a German discothèque owner, Manfred Riek, who had invited the winners of the contests to Majorca for the finals. Clad in bikinis, they had had to spin hula-hoops, do limbo dancing and talk about their hobbies. The applause level had decided the results.

They were a varied lot, from the 16-year-old Simone Liedtke, introduced by Riek as 'my only virgin', to the 36-year-old Jutta Brod, office manager of a village savings bank who had managed to beat her 16-year-old daughter in one of the first rounds. The beauty queens, away from husbands, lovers and friends, had just finished a riotous week. Their farewell party was meant to have ended at 6.30 a.m. For several it had gone on considerably longer. They all arrived only 20 minutes before take-off.

Security checks were as usual for the island airport. The hand luggage was opened, the passengers discreetly patted. The security guards looked into Suhaila Sayeh's light blue make-up case and took note of Akache's large radio set. They noticed nothing. As Hartwig Faby stood in the queue, he suddenly thought he recognized a former colleague – long black hair, dark skin, and unusually large expressive eyes. He was wrong of course; it was Suhaila Sayeh.

A few of the passengers noticed the next figure of Hind Alameh and the strikingly handsome Wabil Harb, dressed in a pastel green suit, his shirt wide open. When Gaby Dillmann welcomed him on board the Landshut with her obligatory smile, she was struck by his good looks.

Akache was noticed only because of his strikingly bright jacket, which did not seem to suit him very well.

The Landshut, with its 86 passengers and five crew members, took off about 11.00 a.m. Vietor was at the controls. In the cabin, the stewardesses began to hand out lunch. The plane was almost fully booked.

After half an hour or so, Schumann and Vietor saw Marseilles in front of them. In the cabin, Gaby Dillmann was getting the trolley ready to clear away the meal, when she saw two figures in the gangway going towards the cockpit. She thought: 'Someone seems to have lost his nerve and somebody's going after him.'

Marseilles was already disappearing beneath the Landshut when Akache tore open the cockpit door. Jürgen Schumann found himself looking down the barrel of a pistol. Vietor heard a movement on his left, tore off his headphones and heard a voice screaming in English, almost incomprehensible with tension: 'Get out! Get out! Get out of the cockpit! Get to the back!'

Vietor retreated into the cabin under a hail of blows and kicks. As he came out he came up against passengers who were being herded, with hands raised, out of the first class compartment into the economy section. Two girls, arms outstretched, with grenades in their hands, were shouting at them. Akache came out of the cockpit. He kicked and struck people, screaming threats about opening fire.

All the crew members (except Schumann) and the passengers from the front part of the cabin were driven together into the rear.

Vietor murmured over and over again, loud enough for those standing near him to hear, that the first rule during a hijacking was to do everything you were told.

A child began to cry. An old woman collapsed. Gaby Dillmann took down her hands and knelt down to her. The chief stewardess, Hannelore Piegler, whispered: 'Have you gone mad, do you want to be shot? Put your hands up!' Gaby Dillmann stood up again, leaving the old woman on the floor.

Akache went to the microphone and screamed into it so loudly that his words were distorted into incomprehensibility. He called Gaby Dillmann over. She remembered that she had brought him his food and had exchanged a couple of sentences in English with him. 'Hey! Air-hostess!' he ordered, 'Translate!'

Gaby Dillmann said: 'You have to speak softly into the microphone, otherwise nobody will understand anything.'

Akache looked at her in surprise, then tried to lower his voice. He was scarcely able to control himself. 'This is Captain Martyr Mahmud speaking. The plane is under my command, whoever does not follow my instructions will be shot immediately.'

Gaby Dillmann translated into German as much as she could understand: *'Hier spricht Captain Martyr Machmud. . . .'*

Then the stewardess added something on her own initiative: *'Tun Sie, was Captain Machmud sagt.'* ('Do whatever Captain Mahmud says.')

More orders followed, Akache – or Mahmud as he now called himself – told the passengers on pain of instant execution to hold their hands up, close the blinds, throw all their knives into the gangway and keep silent. He then ordered the older women to collect up the trays and stack them in the first class section.

Lilo Cramer pressed herself down into her seat. She tried not to look at any of the kidnappers. She thought over and over again: 'They're going to find out that you're Jewish. They're going to shoot you.'

Suddenly Mahmud was standing before her and shouting: 'What's up with you? Come on! come on!'

Lilo Cramer tried to control the trembling. She stood up and tried to take the tray of a very old man, but he held it tight and said loudly: 'What do you think you're doing? I haven't finished eating!' He clearly had no idea what was happening. Suhala Sayeh came over to Lilo Cramer, held a hand grenade in front of her face and shouted: 'Don't move! Not a word!'

Eventually Gaby managed to make clear that the old man had not understood the situation. She managed to take the tray herself.

Mahmud warned: 'If anyone retains any weapons, they'll be shot.'

The men were ordered to come singly into the gangway to be searched. Mahmud seized a nailfile from the boxing promoter, Hans Heyn, screamed, 'What's this? It's a weapon!' pressed the barrel of his 9-mm Makarow against Heyn's breast and hit him across the face with the flat of his left hand.

The passengers were then told to throw down all their papers and any 'Zionist' goods. Mahmud repeated his threat: 'If I find any of this type of thing later, the guilty people will be executed on the spot.'

A Lufthansa employee from Berlin, Birgit Röhll, who had been separated from her ten-year-old son Stefan, tucked her Lufthansa pass into her bra. She was not on duty and had a vague fear that the pass would give her a separate identity, would separate her from the passengers among who she felt relatively safe. Later, she slipped the pass into her handbag.

She pondered the odd chance that had landed her in this situation. She had actually booked on a charter flight, but her name had been left off the passenger list for the return journey by mistake. By the time the error was discovered, the flight was full and she had been placed on the 181 instead.

Next, the terrorists gathered in the hand luggage. Mahmud said with a grin: 'If I find anything else. . . .' Birgitt Röhll realized that it had been a mistake to put her Lufthansa pass into her handbag.

Mahmud repeatedly struck passengers. He did not strike very hard, but his violent outbursts put the hostages into a permanent state of panic and reduced them to a state of shocked paralysis. Suhaila Sayeh screamed orders, always with her arms out, holding grenades in her hands. She had removed the pins, which dangled from her little fingers.

Vietor raised his hand a couple of times like a nervous schoolboy. When Mahmud acknowledged him, he first warned the passengers to follow orders and then asked the hijacker to speak more quietly so that people could understand.

Outwardly Vietor was calm. He was concerned to behave in the way advised by Salewski on the Lufthansa instructional film he had seen – follow orders, but don't be over friendly; no panic; act calm.

Inside, however, he was as frightened as the other passengers. When the attack started, he thought: 'Now you're going to die. Now Renate will be up against it.' Somewhat later, he found his thoughts rambling on: 'We've bought the land in Bensheim. The plans are drawn up. What about the money? We've signed. We have to pay soon. Now Renate's going to be left to handle it. Perhaps she'll go back to the North, to her parents.' Then he began to feel sorry for himself: 'Heavens, you've been through so much military service and now this has to happen. . . .' Then he tried to imagine how Renate would hear of the hijacking: 'She's in school now, so she won't get any news there. So after she gets back, somebody from Lufthansa will call up. . . . No, they wouldn't be so inhuman. They'll send somebody round. . . . She can be very strong. She'll react very practically and know exactly what's happened.'

Lilo Cramer carefully took some jewellery and her purse, containing 5,000 marks, from her handbag. She hid the jewellery in her clothing. 'They're not going to have this,' she thought, 'even if they kill me.' When the terrorists asked for her bag, she ostentatiously put her purse back in. Mahmud took out the purse, opened it and threw it in her lap: 'We don't need your money,' he said. 'Not a penny. Keep it!'

The hostages from the first class section were ordered into the free seats in the economy section. Vietor was told to go back into the cockpit.

There Mahmud ordered Schumann to fly to Cyprus. Schumann pointed out that the fuel might not last out, but he said he could not work out the flying time while he was still at the controls. Vietor did some calculations and found that they had no chance of reaching Cyprus. 'We have to come down in Rome, whatever happens,' he announced.

While LH181 was flying above the Mediterranean, a meeting of the Bonn crisis staff was coming to an end. Schmidt, Interior Minister, Werner Maihofer, Justice Minister, Hans-Jochen Vogel and the President of the Criminal Office had been discussing the Schleyer situation. There were numerous points on the agenda – the results of the manhunt, security, justice, media and the condition of the hostage himself. Experts reported. The team discussed. No one now could see any reason for optimism. Salewski said, and the police agreed with him, that Schleyer would be killed if the conditions were not met or a rescue made. Schleyer had become dangerous – he knew too much about his captors. Besides, according to Baader's thinking, Schleyer's murder would further intensify the crisis and would therefore be necessary.

At 1.10 p.m. the meeting ended. Exactly 88 minutes later, Schmidt's telephone went. It was Maihofer. He said that Flight Control in Aix-en-Provence had reported that LH181 had changed course. 'It looks like a hijacking,' he concluded.

As the Landshut neared Rome, Mahmud sent Vietor back to sit with the passengers. Mahmud took the co-pilot's seat. He clearly knew that the 737 could be flown by one pilot without difficulty. He seemed still very excited and continuously threatened the captain with his pistol. Schumann brought the Landshut safely down at Rome's Fiumicino Airport. He was ordered to halt a thousand yards from the airport buildings. There, armoured cars encircled the plane.

Mahmud reached for the microphone. Again he shouted into it so loudly that those in the tower could hardly understand him. From his long tirade in English, the Italians gleaned his demands: 'The group I represent demand the release of our comrades held in German prisons. We are fighting against the world's imperialist organizations.'

Shortly afterwards, these few sentences were read through to Maihofer. He had himself put through to an Italian colleague, the Christian Democrat Interior Minister Francesco Cossiga, and told him that even on the scanty information available the hijackers seemed to be involved somehow with the Schleyer kidnapping. The plane had to be kept where it was. Maihofer suggested to Cossiga that the tyres should be shot out.

Cossiga said he would have to speak to a colleague before any military action could be initiated. He seemed more appalled at the hijacking than Maihofer. Perhaps he was remembering the fate of his predecessor, Emilio Taveani, who resigned after 34 people had been killed during a battle with Palestinian hijackers in December 1973. The colleague Cossiga turned to was not a Christian Democrat but a Communist. Using the special telephone link set up to allow top Italian politicians to speak to each other in private, he called the Secretary of the Italian Communist Party, Enrico Berlinguer.

He did so for both political and personal reasons. The Christian Democratic government had the tacit support of the Communists and could not act in such desperate circumstances without their approval. But in addition Cossiga and Berlinguer were cousins and both of them came from Sardinia.

Berlinguer was also horrified at the thought of another battle with Palestinians. He already had enough trouble with the younger members of his Party and with extreme Leftists who sympathized with radical Palestinians. The two rapidly agreed that the sooner the German plane left, the better.

It could be that their decision saved lives, for Maihofer's demand to shoot out the Landshut's tyres was taken without consulting Schmidt or the other members of the crisis staff. The police and Salewski were appalled when they heard of Maihofer's proposal. A Criminal Office official commented later: 'If the tyres had been shot out, the man inside would have known that he could not have got away. From then on the situation could only have escalated. The only way forward was to give the impression of cooperation.'

Salewski once again emphasized his own approach: 'Never react abruptly. Always try to reduce tension. Never make demands.'

In the Landshut, the crew felt the same way. They feared that any action seen by Mahmud as aggressive would drive him to fulfil his threats. Schumann therefore backed Mahmud's demand that the plane should be refuelled. He asked for and received a weather report for Cyprus, and got landing permission. A tanker drove out to the plane.

Vietor was allowed back into the cockpit. Schumann suggested that Vietor took the controls. Schumann would then be free to navigate and communicate with Mahmud. It was a good suggestion. Vietor had some three years more flying experience on the 737 than Schumann, who had already had some experience in reasoning with the Palestinian.

Schumann requested clearance for take-off. The reply was evasive: 'Well, we have to keep airspace free. There are planes landing and taking off. It will take a little time.'

Mahmud, who had calmed down a little, became nervous again. Suddenly he shouted: 'Take off now! Immediately!'

Schumann and Vietor were somewhat at a loss. All their training told them that to ignore air traffic control would lead to catastrophe. But a look at Mahmud brandishing his pistol convinced them. 'Okay, will do,' said Schumann. At 5.45 p.m. the Landshut took off for Cyprus.

In Bonn an inner circle of the crisis staff were meeting once again. At first, Schmidt let the meeting take its own course. But the ministers and security experts seemed helpless.

Schmidt began to tap idly on his snuff box. The talk petered out. Schmidt told them his decision. Even after the hijacking of the Lufthansa, there would be no giving in. The R.A.F. prisoners would not be released.

The Chancellor asked his colleagues to take a number of things into account. If the prisoners were released, an unknown number of people would be endangered. The imprisoned terrorists had already killed 13 people and attempted to kill another 43. The Lorenz case showed what would happen: five terrorists had been released; since then, they were known to have been responsible for four murders, were suspected of nine others and were wanted for attempted murder in a further six cases. Besides, the police who were now hunting terrorists at considerable personal risk, would see little point in their work if they knew that any prisoners could be released later.

Next day there was to be a full meeting of the crisis staff at which the Chancellor would explain his hard line. Meanwhile, he did what he could to get additional support. He called French President, Giscard d'Estaing and the British Prime Minister, James Callaghan. Giscard backed Schmidt's decision. Callaghan, who was on a visit to a Coleman's mustard factory in Norwich, asked for an hour's grace. When he called back he said he was completely behind the Chancellor.

Schmidt also told Maihofer to arrange for the élite anti-terrorist unit of the Frontier Force, the *Grenzschutzgruppe*-9 (GSG-9), to trail the Landshut.

Schmidt was quite ready to have GSG-9 mount an assault on foreign soil, but he let another day go by before he officially decided to place the lives of the hostages – and of West Germany's international prestige – in the hands of the young commandos.

In Bensheim, Renate Vietor came back from school at 5.30 p.m. She called up some parents and pupils. A few minutes after she had finished, the telephone went. It was a woman from Lufthansa who said in a friendly way that she had to report 'some changes which would affect her husband.'

'What are you talking about?' replied Renate.

'Well, perhaps you had better sit down first,' said the friendly voice. 'The plane your husband is on has been hijacked.'

After a pause, Renate, controlled and practical, said she wanted to know exactly what had happened. Finally she asked: 'And where is my husband at this moment?'

'They have just taken off from Rome.'

At Frankfurt Airport, in the office that managed the staff of Lufthansa's 707 fleet, Rüdeger von Lutzau was having coffee and cakes with some colleagues. Somebody came into the room and said, almost jokingly: 'Heard the latest? 181 has been hijacked.'

Rüdeger stood up: 'You don't want to make jokes like that,' he said, 'my friend Gaby's on it.' He soon learned that it was no joke.

He went to his department head and said: 'If you want to send a 707 after it and need a co-pilot, send me.' His boss agreed.

The Landshut was approaching Crete. As they crossed the island, another Lufthansa plane, going in the opposite direction, radioed them. Mahmud picked up the microphone and controlling his voice better than before said: 'Here is Captain Martyr Mahmud from the Kaffre Gadum Operation of the Halimeh Commando, fighting against the imperialist organizations of the world.'

The pilot of the other plane said once or twice: 'I don't quite understand,' and then broke contact.

The weather had closed in, but Vietor landed safely at Larnaca at 8.28 p.m. The tower told him to turn around and taxi to the furthest end of the runway. He asked for fuel. He was told he would have to wait: the tanker's crew were at home in Nicosia and would have to be fetched.

After an hour or so, a representative of the P.L.O. came on the radio. First in English, then in Arabic, he tried to persuade Mahmud to let the hostages go.

Mahmud responded with his worst outbreak so far. He screamed in Arabic, leapt about the cockpit and threw the microphone against the mountings. It did not break. The P.L.O. representative gave up.

A tanker came up. The plane was refuelled.

As the tanker withdrew, Schumann passed on Mahmud's orders to flight control: 'We're flying to Beirut.'

After a few minutes, the tower replied: 'Beirut is closed. The airport is blocked.'

Schumann insisted, with the same reply.

Eventually Mahmud said: 'Let's go. If we can't go to Beirut we'll go to Damascus.'

At 10.50 p.m. the Landshut took off again, heading for Beirut. There, the airport told them yet again: 'The airport is blocked.' They flew over Beirut and on towards Damascus. There again they were told: 'The airport is blocked. You can't land here.'

'Okay. Then we'll go to Baghdad,' said Mahmud. It too was blocked. On the Landshut went to Kuwait. Blocked. Schumann had set the device with which all large planes are equipped and which puts out a signal picked up by ground radar – to transmit the international call-sign for a hijacked aircraft.

Schumann also sent out emergency calls to other planes. A Qantas flight replied, the pilot asked if they could help. Schumann replied: 'We're running out of fuel. Could you try and get us landing permission in Kuwait?'

A little later the Qantas pilot replied: 'Sorry, they are adamant. Why don't you try Bahrain or Dahran?'

'We'll try Bahrain,' Mahmud announced.

Schumann could not raise Bahrain. He asked the Qantas pilot to try it. After a few minutes the Australian replied: 'Bahrain is blocked.' Then Schumann made contact for himself. The controller was clearly English. He repeated emphatically and with apparently genuine sympathy: 'I am really *terribly* sorry, the airport is blocked.'

'We haven't got the fuel to go anywhere else,' said Schumann, in desperation.

Mahmud had become extremely edgy again: 'Land now!' he said, 'I don't care how or where! But go down immediately!'

Schumann told Bahrain control that they had to land.

Bahrain replied: 'Bahrain is blocked. We're sorry, but the officials refuse to give you landing permission.'

Then, to Schumann's surprise, the controller announced the frequency on which to make an automatic landing before repeating, 'Sorry, the airport is blocked.'

But now Schumann and Vietor knew for certain that they could land. There was only one runway open for automatic landings; and if the signal was being transmitted, that runway at least was not blocked.

Vietor circled the city, made his approach on automatic and landed normally. It was 1.52 a.m. Vietor cut his engines in the far corner of the air-field.

Mahmud seized the microphone again: 'This is Captain Martyr Mahmud,' he announced, 'of the Kaffre Gadum Operation. . . .'

The tower did not understand. Schumann and Vietor explained what the Palestinian had said.

In the cabin the passengers were relieved that Mahmud remained out of sight. By now the hostages had had a chance to come to some conclusions about the hijackers. Most had classified them as either 'good' or 'bad'. Mahmud was definitely bad, but nobody could decide whether he was crazy or whether his sadistic outbursts were carefully calculated. Suhaila Sayeh was bad, too. She was doing the terrorists' heavy work. For 12 hours, she had stood in the gangway with her two hand grenades. She shouted at any passenger who said anything or moved. Some saw hate in her eyes, others only excitement. She was a bit fatter than her female accomplice. Her jeans and blouse appeared too tight for her. They called her 'the fat one'.

Most reckoned that the slim, quiet and attractive Hind Alameh was good. She became animated only when Mahmud told her to do something. She seemed to follow his every movement with admiration. When Mahmud was not in the cabin, her face became expressionless, her eyes moving dully over the passengers. They referred to her as 'the small one'.

Almost nobody feared Wabil Harb, 'the young one', as he was nicknamed by the passengers. He was the only one who ever talked to the passengers in a friendly way. He spoke English, French and a little German. Lilo Cramer was afraid of him however: 'He's like the ones you see in Italian films.

He's a killer, as slippery as an eel. They've got no brain, they're just killers. Good looking, quiet, nice, sympathetic they just carry out their orders.'

Lilo Cramer thought she was going blind that night. Since the war, she had had a glaucoma. She could only see clearly through one eye and had to take eye-drops regularly. In case she was ever unconscious she had a card, detailing her medical requirements. She showed the card to Gaby Dillmann who was sitting beside her and whispered: 'The drops are in my handbag. If I don't get it back soon, I'll go blind. It's particularly dangerous when I get excited.'

Gaby Dillmann was horrified. Although no one was allowed to move, she stood up and went over to Hind Alameh, 'the small one', and explained the situation. Hind Alameh waved Lilo Cramer over to the first class section where the handbags lay. She said: 'Find your handbag, then, quickly.' Lilo Cramer involuntarily touched the terrorist. She began to tremble, and then to cry.

'Why are you crying?' the small one asked, irritated.

Lilo Cramer replied: 'Because I was afraid that you wouldn't allow me to fetch my drops.'

'Why shouldn't I allow it?' the small one shouted suddenly. 'For God's sake, take your drops and sit down!'

Gaby Dillmann had been called over to Mahmud to translate something. Lilo Cramer found the drops and went back to her place. She was trembling so much she could hardly hold the little bottle. She made a number of vain attempts to get some drops into her eye.

Suddenly the small one was standing beside her. 'What is the matter?' she asked.

'I want Gaby to come and put some drops into my eye,' Lilo Cramer replied. 'I haven't got a mirror, and my hands are trembling so much I can't manage it on my own.'

The small one put her hand-grenade on to the floor, put the safety catch of her pistol on, and stuck the pistol into her hip pocket. Then she pushed Lilo Cramer's head back with her left hand and used her right hand to put a few drops into her eyes.

Lilo Cramer said: 'Thank you.'

The small one lifted up her hand grenade again without

saying a word, pulled her pistol out of her pocket and clicked the safety catch off again.

Suddenly the crew saw that the Landshut was surrounded by soldiers. Mahmud became frightened and pointed his pistol at Vietor's head. He shouted into the microphone: 'If your soldiers haven't gone in five minutes time, I am going to shoot the pilot.' He took his watch off, laid it on the arm of Vietor's seat and repeated: 'In five minutes, you're dead if the soldiers haven't gone.'

One minute later, he pressed the button and said into the microphone: 'Four minutes to go.'

Schumann began to talk quietly to the Palestinian: 'You can't do that. I can't fly without him. It's madness. The tower has no communication with the soldiers. How can they be told to leave within five minutes?'

'Three minutes to go,' said Mahmud.

Vietor began to plead for his life. He asked to be allowed to speak to the tower.

Mahmud gave him the microphone.

Vietor shouted and begged, almost crying: 'He's going to shoot me! Please call your soldiers off! Please, please, please!'

As he spoke, he lowered his head on to his chest, but the barrel of the pistol remained trained on his temples.

'A minute to go,' said Mahmud, and then: 'Thirty seconds to go.'

At that moment Schumann shouted: 'They're moving! Captain Mahmud! Look! They really are moving!'

Vietor shouted: 'Don't shoot! They're moving!'

The soldiers withdrew slowly into the darkness. The Palestinian lowered his pistol.

Later the plane was refuelled. Mahmud said: 'Now we're going to Dubai.' Schumann read out the check-list. Vietor turned the plane round, still in a state of shock, reacting automatically. There was a light wind. Vietor took off normally into the clear, star-lit night.

Back in Hangelaar, near Cologne, at the HQ of GSG-9, the telephone rang. It was an Interior Ministry official asking for the GSG-9 commander, Ulrich Wegener. His deputy, Klaus Blätte, went to the phone. The man from the Interior Ministry asked: 'Have you heard about the hijacking?' Blätte said he had.

'The Minister wants you to prepare to storm the aircraft and free the hostages.' Confirmation would follow later, he said.

Blätte could hardly believe his ears: after five years of training, action at last!

They were certainly ready for it. In those five years, they had become experts in karate, in shooting with a wide variety of guns, and in blowing up and defusing bombs. Their multi-million mark budget had supplied them with specially equipped Mercedes limousines, armoured cars, heavy motor cycles and a helicopter fleet. They had trained in storming planes. They knew how to get inside many western makes in seconds, having practised on mock ups. Russian planes might have given a little more trouble because they had nothing to practise on; but they knew all the details of the Russian makes, for the security-conscious Russians had provided them with plans.

They had already had enough of a reputation to warrant some action. The commander of the Israeli Border Patrol, Zvi War, had called GSG-9 'The best anti-terrorist group in the world.' The Israelis knew what they were saying because Wegener, 46, trained with them. So impressed were they with him that they had invited him along as an observer at the Entebbe raid.

But so far GSG-9 had been kept in reserve. There had been occasions on which their skills would have been useful, but *Land* governments had been shy of bringing in the commandos over their own police. Understandably, Wegener had thought of resigning. There was no point, he thought, in training a team only to keep them out of action.

At 7.42 p.m. Maihofer called Wegener. He told him that the decision had officially been made. Thirty men were to prepare for departure.

An hour later Wegener told the men he had selected what was expected of them. He was as forthcoming and as exact as he could be: 'Accurate information,' he believes, 'is part of motivation.' Wegener told his men that they had a hard nut to crack. He reminded them of the difficulties of storming an aircraft: 'Even the approach is dangerous. There's no cover. Everything happens in a narrow space. You never know how the hijackers or the hostages are going to react. Sometimes you can't tell the difference between passengers and hijackers. And shooting not only risks lives unnecessarily – it can put holes in leads and fuel tanks.'

He spoke of a 'suicide mission'. He said he would not blame anybody for stepping down. The men grinned.

There was one problem: the three unit leaders Schmidt, Weigolt and Tütter, all wanted to come, but only one was needed. Wegener suggested: 'Let's decide things between us.' Schmidt withdrew of his own accord: 'Nothing will come of it,' he said, 'we'll never get to attack and I'll only be angry if we come back without even seeing the hijacked plane.' The other two decided to toss for it. Tütter spun a five-mark piece. Weigolt called: 'Heads,' and won. Tütter was a bad loser: 'It's unbelievable,' he complained. 'Every year I win at practise and now I have to stay behind.'

Besides Weigolt and Wegener there was Wegener's adjutant, Baum, two explosives experts, a communications technician and 24 rank and file members – 30 people in all.

They took with them their personal weapons, 100 hand grenades, ladders and enough explosive to put the plane out of commission. Baum also brought along as many details as he could about Boeing 737's.

At 9.45 p.m. the group was ready at Cologne-Bonn airport. They looked like a sports team – young men in track-suits, gym-shoes, jeans and pullovers.

At 10.13 p.m. they were ready for take-off in a Boeing 737, destined for Cyprus, where the Landshut was at that moment still waiting to be refuelled. The team was in a holiday mood.

Shortly before they landed in Cyprus – a few minutes before the hijacked plane left at 10.50 p.m. (local time) – the captain came back and said to Wegener: 'It's odd, but the tower has just asked me who we had on board. I said German experts. Better pack away your hardware.'

After touchdown, Cyprus's Police Chief came on board.

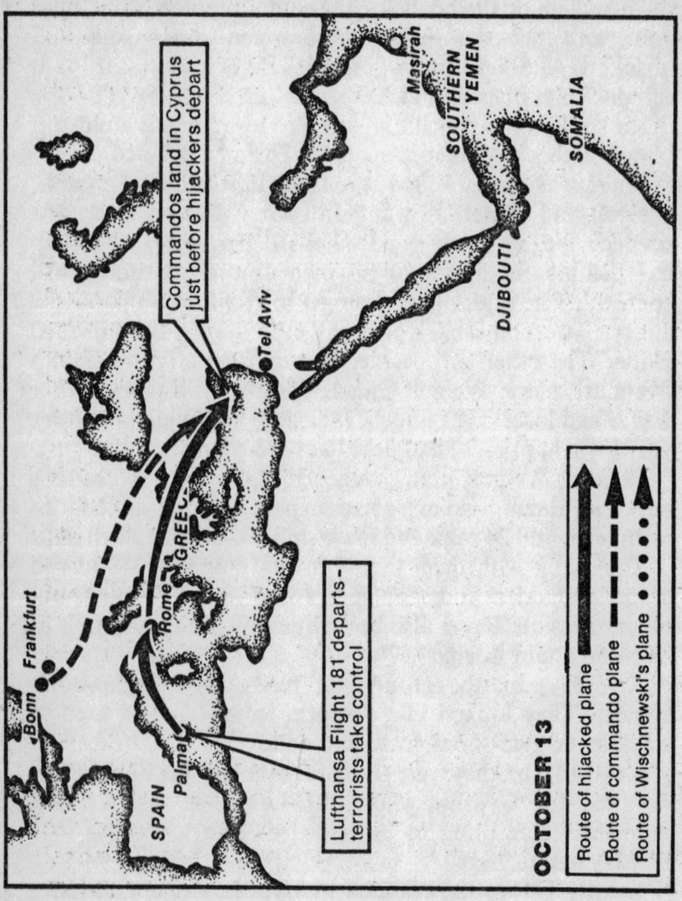
Commandos land in Cyprus just before hijackers depart
Masirah
SOUTHERN YEMEN
SOMALIA
DJIBOUTI
Tel Aviv
Frankfurt
Bonn
Rome
GREEC
SPAIN
Palma
Lufthansa Flight 181 departs - terrorists take control
OCTOBER 13
Route of hijacked plane
Route of commando plane
Route of Wischnewski's plane

He looked over the passengers. Some were playing cards, many gave him a friendly grin.

A little later the order came through that the 'German specialists' were to leave Cyprus as soon as possible.

Then came the news that the hijackers had already left. There followed a message from the German Interior Ministry: 'Return to Cologne immediately.'

The plane took off at about 4.00 a.m. Soon afterwards it was redirected to Ankara.

Early on Friday, October 14, Payot's office in Geneva contacted the Criminal Office with a message from the hijackers. It read in part: 'The lives of the passengers and crew and the life of Hanns Martin Schleyer depend on the fulfilment of the following demands.' These were identical with the kidnappers' demands – the terrorists' names were even in the same order – but with additions. The hijackers wanted the release of two Palestinians – 'Mahdi' and 'Hussein' – imprisoned in Turkey, plus 15 million dollars. The deadline was set for 9.00 a.m. on Sunday, the 16th. The message was signed by 'The Struggle Against World Imperialists Organizations', a previously unknown name.

Another message relayed by Payot at the same time was from the 'Kaffre Gadum' operation, which named the hijackers as 'our Martyr Halimeh Commando', as Mahmud had done. It claimed unity with the Siegfried Hausner commando in the fight against Neo-Nazism, Zionism and imperialism – views identical to those later expressed by Mahmud.

These statements made the link between the two operations abundantly clear. This was not surprising since West German terrorists were known to have trained with Palestinians and there was enough similarity between the messages and Mahmud's demands – vague and hysterical though they were – to assume a definite link. But the nature of the link was not – and is not – clear. How much of a joint operation were the two crimes? How could the messages have been directly from the hijackers, who were in the Landshut at the time? Was the message sent by the Schleyer kidnappers? If so, it might account for Mahmud's vagueness – the only time he mentioned the terrorist prisoners, he referred only to nine not 11; and he seemed oddly unaware of the October 16 deadline.

DUBAI

Schumann picked up the Dubai tower. He asked for permission to land. After a pause, there came the reply: 'The airport is blocked. Sorry.'

With the help of the flight plan, Schumann indicated the holding pattern to his co-pilot and the plane began to circle at 8,000 feet. The pilots looked out at the moonless, starlit sky. They relaxed. The fuel would last a while yet. There would be a bit of a pause before the next unavoidable decision. Vietor asked Schumann to take the controls, lay back and napped for half an hour. Several more times, Schumann asked for permission to land. The reply was the same: 'Sorry; the runway is blocked.'

Mahmud sat hunched up in the observer's seat in the cockpit. Occasionally he started out of his lethargy, tore the microphone from Vietor's hand and poured out a stream of Arabic. The tower seemed not to understand him. He kept on repeating the same phrase, over and over again.

At last a streak of red sky in the east signalled the coming of dawn. The edge of the sun appeared, shimmering in the haze, at the distant edge of the sand dunes. The pilots saw that the landing strip was blocked by a number of planes. Sheik Rashid, Dubai's ruler, had ordered fire engines on to the runways.

From the cockpit, no movement could be seen in the airport. In the pale light of morning, the place looked dead. Schumann and Vietor looked for a clear strip of concrete on which they could land. There was only one place: the taxi-way. They estimated its length.

Schumann said, 'Sometime we are going to run out of juice. We have to land somewhere. Perhaps we'll be in luck.' Then he felt a pistol in the back of his neck. Mahmud shouted from behind, 'You'll go down now!' and shifted the barrel up to Vietor's temple. 'You'll land now! Now! You'll land now!'

'There's no arguing with that,' muttered Vietor under his breath.

Schumann turned round to Mahmud and tried to explain calmly, 'We have to go down to a lower level first . . .'

'You will land now!'

'. . . to see where we can land best.'

'Okay,' replied the Palestinian, more quietly, and lowered his pistol.

Schumann radioed the tower: 'We have to come in now. We're landing,' giving no reason for his announcement.

He told the stewardess to prepare for an emergency landing. It was 5.40, local time.

In their first pass over the airport, the men noticed that the fire engines were pulling back. The airport commander had taken the initiative to move them, without waiting for Sheik Rashid's orders. He clearly wanted to avoid a disaster.

Vietor brought the machine down as lightly as if he had been on a routine flight.

As the aircraft rolled to a halt, Mahmud seized the microphone again. Screaming shrilly, he introduced himself as 'The leader of the Martyr Halimeh Commando.'

'The machine is under our complete control,' he shouted. 'If you don't follow our orders, the aeroplane will be blown up.' In Arabic he explained the demands of the Commando. Then he asked for refreshments to be brought to the plane.

The airport commander got in contact with the palace of the Defence Minister of the United Arab Emirates, Sheik Mohammed bin Rashid. The Sheik had gone out for a morning tour of his private zoo. On this particular Friday – the Arab's Sabbath – he was preparing to go falconing. The Defence Minister clearly thought that he had earned some relaxation, for the previous evening he had returned from a tiring mission to South Lebanon, where he had vainly tried to organize a ceasefire between the Palestinian and Christian forces.

Sheik Mohammed, who was just 29 years old and the third son of Dubai's ruler, ordered his driver to take him to the airport. The car swept along the open road at 120 miles an hour. One of Mohammed's hobbies is fast cars.

As a soldier, Mohammed, Sandhurst-trained, had had some experience of situations like this. It was the fourth hijacking he had handled in Dubai, and the previous three had been brought to a successful conclusion.

Sheik Mohammed was to remain in the airport's command post for the next three days and two nights, taking only the occasional short nap wrapped in a woollen blanket on the floor. The Sheik immediately established contact with Mahmud in the cockpit of the Landshut. He asked the hijacker to release the women, the children and the sick. He spoke with him 'as an Arab brother' to no avail. He tried ordering him. Finally, from the occasional phrases that he could understand, the Defence Minister realized that there would be no compromise. 'There is nothing to be done at the moment,' the young Sheik said, 'The man is very nervous. I think he is sick.'

In the cabin of the Landshut the atmosphere became a little calmer. It was something of a relief for the hostages that Mahmud, involved with the radio, was not to be seen.

The young man and the two girls relieved each other on watch. They no longer kept hand grenades and pistols threateningly on show. The passengers, who had been ordered to hold their hands up or put them on their heads, were allowed to bring them down. The terrorists allowed low conversation.

The blinds remained closed. The passengers had no idea where they were. Except for the children and the elderly, no one had slept the previous night. A few began to doze.

Water was handed out, a mouthful for everybody. One of the girls explained, 'Just dampen your throats, we haven't got any more to drink and we don't know when we will get anything.'

When the stewardess, Gaby Dillmann, went through the cabin, she noticed that everyone touched her arm. A 14-year-old girl looked up at her, blushing, and muttered, 'I've gone in my pants.' Gaby said: 'It really doesn't matter. Take your pants off and we'll hang them somewhere to dry.'

For almost 17 hours the passengers had not been allowed to move from their seats. Now, one by one, they were

THE VICTIM

Hanns-Martin Schleyer, 62, the tough but direct head of West Germany's two most powerful business associations. As a former SS officer and top businessman, he was an obvious target for a terrorist attack. His kidnapping on September 5 hardened the resolve of the West German government never to give in to terrorist demands; thus precipitating, in turn, the hijacking, the assault at Mogadishu, Schleyer's own murder and the prison suicides of the three Baader-Meinhoff leaders.

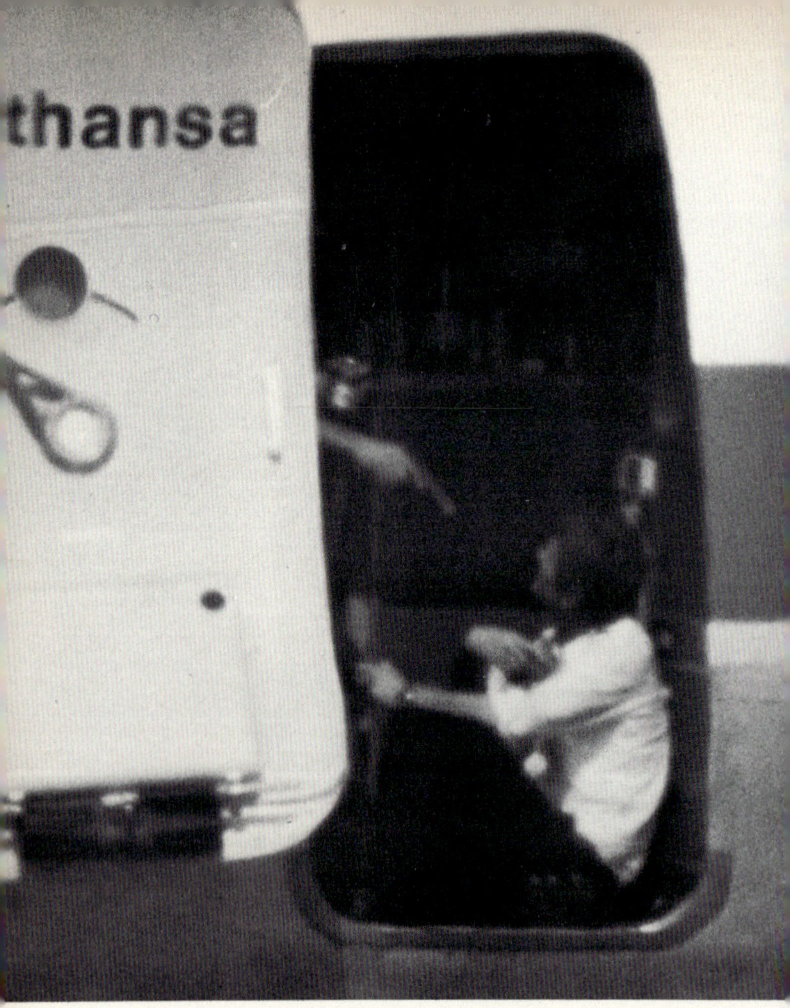

REHEARSAL FOR DEATH
Saturday October 15 Dubai; a gun held by Chief Terrorist 'Captain Mahmoud' is pointed at Captain Jürgen Schumann's head. The door is open to reduce the 105° heat of the interior. The gesture was a joke in a moment of relaxation – but on the following day, Mahmoud shot Schumann.

THE STARFIGHTERS
Ulrich Wegener (above) 46 the wiry head of the GSG-9 Group of about 180 men who had trained for five years for such an occasion. Their training included such unorthodox skills as picking locks and impersonating officials, as well as rigorous tests of unarmed combat (left), shooting, knife fighting, climbing and swimming.

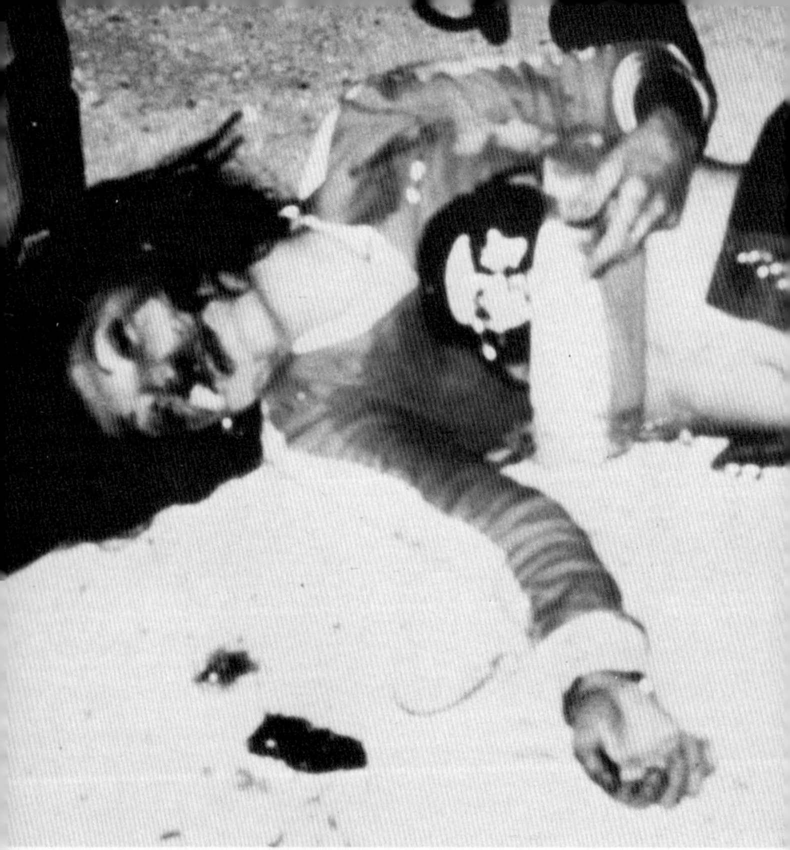

DEATH AND DEFIANCE
In a Che Geuvarra shirt, one of the three terrorists slain in the raid lies on the tarmac at Mogadishu.

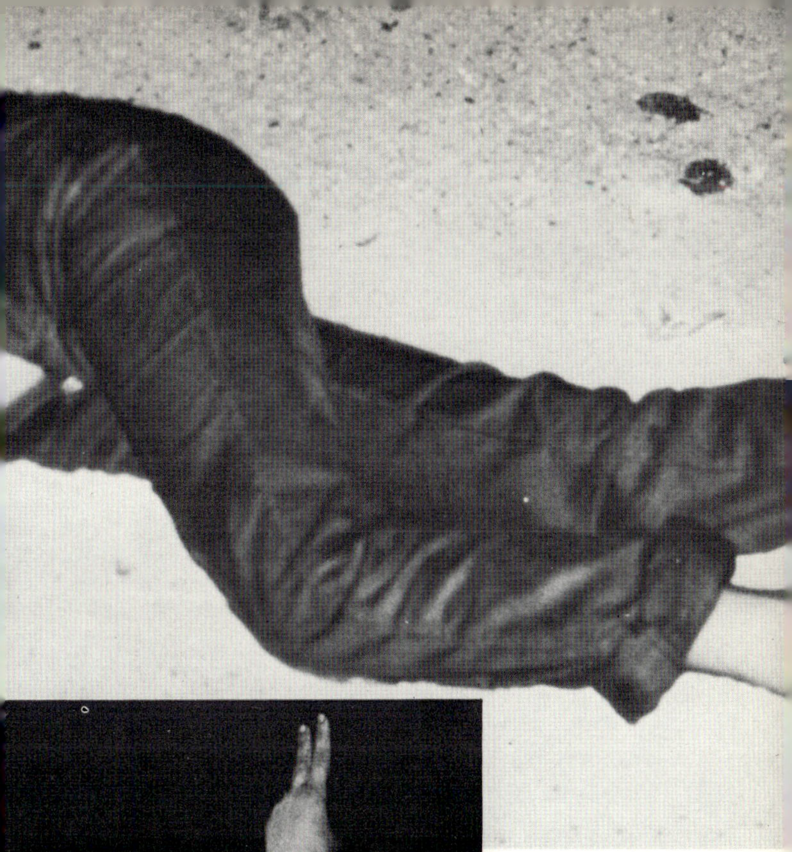

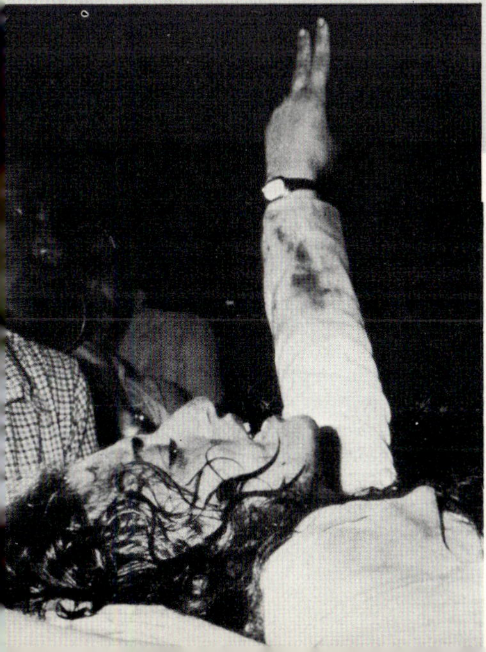

From the surviving, but severely wounded, woman terrorist a defiant victory sign and a scream of Palestine, Palestine.

THE THREE MINUTE VICTORY
In a reconstruction of the assault, lights explode over the front of the plane in a diversionary tactic to keep the terrorists in the cockpit while GSG-9 men approach from the rear to blow open the doors, cut down the terrorist rapid fire and release the passengers.

D-ABCE
D-ABCE
BOEING 737

Andreas Baader

Jan Carl Raspe

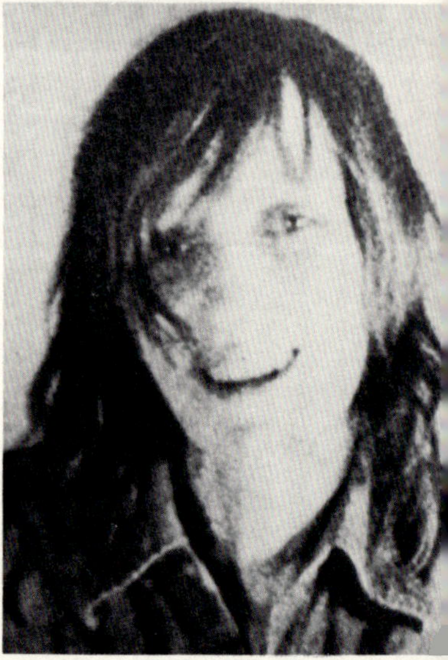

Gudrun Ensslin

PRISON SUICIDES

The three imprisoned Baader-Meinhoff terrorists – Andreas Baader, Gudrun Ensslin and Jan-Carl Raspe – who committed suicide in Stammheim prison when they heard of the successful assault.

allowed to go to the toilet.

The Palestinians vanished, one after another, and reappeared in a change of clothing. They wore smart red T-shirts with white borders, bearing a picture of Che Guevara.

Mahmud called Gaby Dillmann into the first class section. He indicated the somewhat creased portrait on his chest and asked, 'Do you know him?'

'Che Guevara.'

'And do you know what he did?'

'I think so,' said Gaby, 'when I was younger, I had a picture of him in my room, because I found him so good-looking. Later I took it down.'

Then she remembered the company's instructions in case of a hijacking: 'Don't engage in political discussions.'

Mahmud asked: 'Do you know anything about Israel, Persia, Brazil, Chile – what do you know about Chile?'

Gaby said: 'What happened in Chile . . . it was tragic.'

Mahmud's voice became hoarse. Beginning softly, and working himself up, he said, 'A tragedy, you call it – a tragedy when fascists torture democrats – murder by the tens of thousands. A tragedy . . .' He was screaming now, 'Okay! okay! okay! – a tragedy!'

Gaby Dillmann realized that she had touched a raw nerve. She reminded herself, 'No political discussions' and backtracked.

Trying to seem more naive than frightened, she said: 'I know it's bad not to be more interested in politics. I don't know anything about Chile. I haven't any idea. I have to get more involved.'

At that moment, Hind Alameh, who had been listening to the conversation, motionless, knocked against a stack of trays on one of the seats. Plastic plates, knives and forks, and the remains of meals crashed on to the floor. Gaby said quickly 'Bingo!'

Mahmud asked, 'What is Bingo?'

Gaby, grateful that the crashing trays had relieved the tension, replied, 'I always say Bingo when something falls down, if it's an ordinary sort of a crash. It's for luck.'

The Palestinians laughed. Mahmud put away his pistol in his hip pocket. 'Soon we'll play Bingo with the aeroplane,' he said, and from then on the Palestinians said 'Bingo' whenever they made a reference to blowing the passengers up.

Gaby, seeing how delighted the terrorists were to be able to threaten death with such a playful word, promised herself never to say 'Bingo' again.

Mahmud ordered water, food, cigarettes and medicine, in particular throat tablets and some cough medicine for himself. In the tower, they thought that a terrorist who was worried about his throat wasn't seriously thinking of dying. But in the aeroplane, they knew differently. Mahmud had to do something for his voice in order to remain comprehensible at all.

Some Pakistani labourers arrived with bottles of mineral water. They placed them nervously on a step at the front of the plane. The kidnappers were jumpy. They clearly feared some sort of a trick or some sudden movement by the passengers. They raised their pistols, unclicked the safety catches and threatened both the Pakistanis and the passengers with hand grenades.

When the plastic bottles were lifted on board, Mahmud's suspicions seemed to dwindle. He allowed a catering truck to come up to provide food and take away the refuse. Schumann and Vietor, who were supposed to talk to each other in English, risked muttering a few German sentences together.

'We have to tell them something,' said Schumann. 'Do you think it's sensible to try to smuggle something out in the rubbish?'

Vietor replied: 'I don't think that they will look through the rubbish.'

The hijackers wanted newspapers. Schumann muttered to Vietor in German: 'Order four papers, *four*.'

Vietor said in English into the microphone: 'Please send us four English papers, I repeat, four English papers.'

Mahmud noticed nothing.

Schumann wrapped four cigarettes together and threw them into the refuse can. Gaby Dillmann, who had seen what was going on, stood by the open door and waved. Then she put a fist behind the flat of her other hand and spread out four fingers. Those watching should now at least know the number of hijackers involved.

Later the crew could not think why they had risked a dangerous, unpredictable outburst by Mahmud. No one dared think that the plane would be assaulted. Everyone hoped that Bonn would release the R.A.F. prisoners. But for that, the information about how many terrorists were involved was hardly important.

Mahmud anyway noticed nothing. Like the passengers, he ate for the first time in about 24 hours – chicken, bread, sausage, cheese and dessert.

On the plastic boxes which contained the usual cold meal for medium-range flights were the words, 'Airport Dubai'. The passengers now knew where they were and felt relatively safe to be in a pro-Western oil sheikdom. The hostages took heart, in the firm belief that the government would give in to the terrorists' demands.

The stewardesses and terrorists all gave out cigarettes. Hind Alameh lit them without taking the grenade out of her hand. Allowing it to dangle by its pin from her little finger, she flicked the cigarette lighter with her thumb.

Mahmud expressed some concern about the health of the passengers. Himself a chain smoker, he announced, 'The non-smokers should not be allowed to suffocate in fumes.' Displaying an almost fatherly concern, he told the passengers to swap seats: 'Smokers to the back, the others to the front.'

The Lufthansa employee, Birgit Röhll, from Berlin, was especially thankful for the change. Since the hijacking, she had been separated from her 10-year-old son Stefan. Now she went to him and cradled him in her arms. Stefan was quite calm, although a few tears ran down his cheek. Birgit Röhll comforted him: 'Now everything is going to be all right. Nothing more is going to happen.' Birgit Röhll gave no further thought to the Lufthansa card hidden in her make-up bag and Mahmud's threat to 'execute' anyone who had not given up their papers.

The curtain dividing the first and economy-class sections

was drawn. Only the crew members saw that Mahmud and the small woman were going through the passengers' hand luggage and papers.

Hind Alameh came out of the first class and went along the cabin very slowly, checking the faces. At the last row of seats, she stood beside Birgit Röhll and then said: 'Come with me.' Birgit Röhll, trembling, followed the Palastinian through the curtain.

In the first-class section, Mahmud was standing in front of Birgit's open make-up case. In his hand he held her Lufthansa pass and Mont Blanc fountain-pen case. 'Sit down,' he said, easily. On the seats there lay hand luggage and plastic bags for duty-free goods. Birgit sat on an arm of one of the seats.

Then Mahmud commanded hoarsely, but without shouting: 'On the floor.' Birgit knelt down in front of him.

Mahmud held the fountain-pen case in front of her face, showing her the flap with its white, Mont Blanc star. 'What's that?' he asked.

Birgit knew in advance that her reply would anger him. 'It's a fountain-pen case.'

Mahmud raised his hand, but did not strike her. He pointed to the star and repeated quietly, 'What is that?'

'A trademark.'

Mahmud hit her twice in the face and screamed 'It is a Jewish star!'

He ran through to the economy section, along the gangway to where Stefan was sitting. He asked in English: 'Are you Jews?' Somebody translated.

'No,' Stefan replied emphatically.

Mahmud ran back to Birgit who was still on her knees. He threw the fountain-pen case on the floor, stamped on it and said: 'Never buy Zionist goods again!'

Birgit reeled back to her place, trembling and fighting against tears. Stefan stroked her hand, tried to put his arm around her shoulders and whispered with understanding and in an unusually deep voice, 'Mummy, you don't need to be frightened; I am here.' It struck Birgit, as it struck other passengers later, that the children were the calmest and the strongest in the plane.

Hind Alameh smiled down for a moment at the boy as he leant over his mother to comfort her. It was a completely different expression from the smile with which she habitually followed Mahmud's actions.

Gaby sat down in her place. Beside her sat Lilo Cramer, looking at the floor with a fixed and glassy stare. She suddenly turned her head to Gaby, and whispered, almost inaudibly: 'I have to admit something to you. I am Jewish.' She pressed something into the stewardess's hand. It was a scrap of paper. Wrapped in it was a piece of jewellery. 'I am going to die now,' she whispered, 'but they won't get this. Give it to my husband.'

Lilo Cramer had been the only one in her family to survive the Nazi days. Now she was certain she was going to die. She had often asked herself, just how it was that she was still alive. Now she believed she had the answer: 'To die in this way.' She prayed 'Please God, don't let them torture me, let them kill me quickly.'

She searched her mind for the prayers that had helped when she was hiding in basements and cellars from the Gestapo. She had never been a particularly devout Jew. She could only remember one particular verse: 'Lord God in Heaven, Look down on your people Israel and help them in their need.' She repeated it in German and Hebrew without moving her lips. She then remembered a prayer for the dying and repeated over and over again, 'My ancestors Rachel, Leah and Sarah, take me to you and receive me blessed into Heaven.'

Gaby Dillmann did not feel that she could cope with the situation. As she laboured to find the right words, she thought, 'Its terrible ... for God's sake ... I have got to do something.' Then her old confidence came sweeping back. She took Lilo Cramer's hand and said: 'I know nothing is going to happen to you. I know it for sure. Now just remain calm.' And then for the first and only time during the whole hijacking, she lied. 'I overheard them say that tomorrow three people are to be released,' she said, 'and you are to be one of them.'

Lilo Cramer allowed herself to be calmed. She thought: 'God has sent me a good, brave and innocent being so he cannot want me to die.'

Hind Alameh came to fetch another female passenger. Gaby Dillmann was called into the first-class section to translate, for the woman understood no English.

Mahmud said to her: 'You're Jewish!' and struck her.

She replied imploringly: 'No I'm not, I'm Protestant.'

Mahmud gave his stereotyped reply, 'You're Jewish, admit it!'

Then he asked Gaby: 'Doesn't her passport state which religion she is?'

Gaby replied: 'No, German passports don't say that. In our country religion isn't so important.'

'For us it is very important,' replied Mahmud.

Gaby had needed all her strength to reply. She was pouring with sweat and felt very weak. The 'small one' looked at her and smiled her other, friendly smile for a second. She placed her hand on Gaby's back and lead her out of the first-class compartment.

Back in her seat, Gaby fell into a trance-like sleep, her first in two days. Lilo Cramer put a blanket over her and took her swollen feet in her lap; so Gaby did not hear when a third woman, who had been led into Mahmud, cried out in sudden pain.

Gaby was woken by Mahmud's croaking voice as it came over the loud-speaker: 'The three Jewish witches I've dug out will report at 8 o'clock tomorrow morning for execution.'

Shortly afterwards a relaxed Mahmud came out into the economy section. He handed out some cigarettes and had stewardesses bring water.

It was hard to guess the meaning of Mahmud's outburst. There were indeed Jewish passengers on board: they could be identified by their names and by their Israeli passports. Yet Mahmud selected his 'Jewesses' randomly. The Palestinians, who spoke faultless English, were clearly too intelligent and experienced to see in a Mont Blanc trademark a symbol of Jewishness.

The truth was that Mahmud needed some ready victims.

His actions and reactions were uncontrolled. It became clearer and clearer to the crew members that he needed to whip up crises to release his own inner tension, and that he was not psychologically up to the demands of his undertaking.

Having set up his next drama, Mahmud was calm again. He gave out a few more cigarettes and went back into the cockpit. He sat in the captain's seat and switched on the loud-speaker: 'Silence, please,' he said, 'I have something important to say.' Then he began a speech about the history of the Palestinians, full of facts and dates.

He talked for almost an hour. Gaby Dillmann translated through the microphone by the forward door. The Palestinians, Mahmud said, had lived in their home land by the Jordan for 2,000 years, constantly oppressed by foreign rulers. Three world religions had originated in their land. The adherents had lived in Palestine for centuries in peace. Then the British, in conjunction with 'world imperialism,' had deceived the Palestinians and given the land to the Zionists.

'What would you Germans do,' he asked, 'if foreigners from the whole world came to your country and said – we have a book which says that this place belongs to us? The Germans would fight!'

Mahmud's voice betrayed a dangerous excitement when he spoke about the fight of the Palestinians for their homeland.

Suddenly, a shot rang out.

For several long seconds there was a deathly silence, then Mahmud's voice came over, quietly: 'I am sorry. I will now go on with my speech.'

In his excitement, the hijacker, sitting alone in the cockpit, had pulled the trigger of his pistol. Jürgen Vietor found the bullet later in the co-pilot's chair.

As if calmed by the shot, Mahmud explained why he, as a Palestinian, was co-operating with the Schleyer kidnappers: 'The Zionist regime in Israel is the successor to Nazism. Zionism is the spearhead of imperialism in the Arab world. The Bonn neo-Nazis are its most important allies, together with the Americans. Schleyer is one of those types who once served Hitler's Nazis and today lead the neo-Nazi businesses in Bonn and Tel Aviv. That is why we are fighting, together with our German companions, against world imperialism. That's why we will release the German prisoners from the torture prisons. Either that, or we will die for the German cause, as Germans died for us at Entebbe.'

Some of the hostages had listened. The teacher, Hartwig Faby, felt a twinge of conscience. He had to admit to himself that he knew hardly anything about the history of the Palestinians. He promised himself that if he got out of this, he wouldn't in future be so wrapped up in his own problems, but concern himself more with wider issues, like that of the Palestinians.

Jürgen Vietor felt the same. 'Germany is rich and complaisant,' he thought, 'You read in the papers about the P.L.O. and the Palestinians and then dismiss it. God, I'm only just beginning to realize what it is all about.'

Mahmud came back into the cabin after his speech, wandered along the gangway, and then went back to the microphone: 'Another piece of information: the three Jewesses don't need to report to me tomorrow morning. I am not going to execute them.'

Birgit Röhll had understood hardly anything of his speech. She had been thinking about death. Stefan stroked her continuously and talked to her quietly. Now Hind Alameh came up. She gave Stefan an apple and said: 'Now there is no more need to worry. It really doesn't matter whether you are Jewish or not. Nothing will happen to you.' Later she came back again and gave the boy a fan with palms and bullfighters on it. 'A souvenir from Majorca,' she said, 'so you can keep cool.'

The temperature in the cabin was actually still quite bearable – about 86°F. The air conditioning was on. But the system needed power. That came from the generator and it would last only as long as the fuel held out.

Schumann had worked out how long the fuel would last soon after they landed. There was enough for 12 hours. Sometime that evening, the Landshut would be left without electricity, without cool air, and without light. Schumann was afraid that that would panic Mahmud again. He explained, carefully and in detail, what was going to happen.

Mahmud said: 'So we have got to take on more fuel.'

'You know that the Sheik will give us fuel when the women and children have been released,' replied Schumann.

The hijacker became nervous again. The captain took a risk. He decided to show him what would happen. He switched off the generator for a few seconds. In the darkness, Mahmud said: 'Okay, okay, now we know all about it.'

Exactly two hours later the last pint of fuel ran out. The comforting, reliable hum of the dynamo and the fans stopped. Utter silence fell. It was impenetrably dark.

In the next few seconds, the terrorists had no control over their hostages. Yet it did not occur to anyone to open the doors and run for it. No one dared speak.

Schumann switched to stand-by power, which came from a 24-volt battery powerful enough to give the machine an extra half an hour in the air if the generator broke down in flight. Schumann and Vietor went into the cockpit where, with the help of the handbook, they pulled out the fuses of all those pieces of equipment that were connected to the battery but which were not needed on the ground. They hoped to conserve some electricity for emergency lighting and radio communication. Now they could talk only through 'the No. 1 radio' at the captain's seat.

Neither captain nor co-pilot wondered why they were doing so much to make things easier for the hijackers.

Meanwhile, underneath the nose of the Landshut, three men were squatting. They were Lufthansa Captain, Martin Gäbel, and his colleague, Held, who had arrived shortly before from Ankara via Beirut; and a British Military Advisor in Dubai, Major Temple. In whispers they discussed the possibility of weakening the hijackers' position by switching off the power.

They crawled to the left undercarriage support, where there was a switch with which the generator could be put out of action. But it was not certain whether switching off the current would do much good. It would impose an additional burden on the passengers. When the generator ceased to work of its own accord, the decision was made for them, and they made their way back to the control tower.

In the cabin, the temperature rose minute by minute. Soon it was over 120°F.

The younger women were the first to collapse. Mahmud seemed irritated. He ordered the doors to be opened. The stewardesses dragged two unconscious women to the rear entrance. An old woman protested: 'Extraordinary that the young ones should be first.' She tried to stand up and collapsed in the gangway.

Chaos. The hijackers forgot all their safety precautions. They helped to carry those who had fainted to the doors. They dragged out oxygen bottles. In the first-class section, which until then had been banned to passengers, under the threat of immediate execution, women lay about on hand-luggage, plastic explosive and fuses. A dozen people thronged around the rear door, with little supervision. The tarmac was within jumping distance, yet nobody jumped and ran off into the darkness. It was one of those moments in which the odd feeling of unity between the kidnappers and the hostages prevailed over common sense.

Most of the men stripped off their shirts. The women undid their blouses. Gaby Dillmann said to the passengers: 'Now is not the time for false modesty. Take off what you want.' At the stewardess's suggestion, many stripped off to their underwear.

In the pilot's seat, Mahmud sat at the No. 1 Radio and tried to make himself understood at the tower. That was no simple matter, because the emergency battery was getting weaker and weaker. Mahmud no longer made demands; he begged: 'Bring us fuel, even a hundred litres. We have to keep cool. People are dying in here.'

A fuel tanker drove up, approaching from the right. Two men set about attaching the lead under the wing, in preparation for filling the tank under pressure. Jürgen Vietor opened the cockpit window and called out: 'What are you doing? That won't work. We've no current for refuelling under pressure. You have to do it *over* the wing. You have got to pump in the fuel from above.'

The technicians understood. One of them said: 'You are getting 800 litres.' They began to pump fuel into the right wing, from above. After a minute, it occurred to Vietor, too late, that it would not be much use to him. The generator took its fuel from the left wing tank; there was no electricity to pump fuel from the right wing to the left.

The 800 litres were almost in when Vietor shouted out to the technicians: 'Stop! We need the same amount on the other side, otherwise nothing is going to happen.' They did not understand, or did not want to understand. They rolled up the leads and Vietor saw the tanker's red brake lights disappear behind a sand dune.

Meanwhile, conditions in the cabin had become critical, especially for the older passengers.

The 82-year-old grandfather, who had never shown any sign of understanding what was happening in the Landshut, seemed completely unaffected by the heat and the lack of oxygen. Occasionally, the hostages could hear his strong, clear voice: '*Oma*, where's the torch? I want some light.' At last, his wife said: 'I can't find it, either.' The old man, in a voice befitting a former officer, ordered, 'Then go and get the other one!'

The old lady stood up. She swayed along the gangway towards the rear door. There she collapsed. Wabil Harb ran to her. He put down his torch and those behind saw that he had put his pistol in his back pocket and laid his hand-grenade beside him. He turned the old woman carefully on her back.

The teacher, Hartwig Faby, saw a man jump up. It was a passenger whose nerve had clearly snapped. The man shouted: 'Not like that!' Faby ducked down in his seat. He was certain that the man was going to seize the hijacker's weapon and attack him. Faby was one of those few on board who continuously rehearsed in his mind the possibility of such an attack. He had dismissed all his plans because he believed that none of the passengers would go along with him. Now, when somebody actually seemed to be making a move, he was paralysed with horror.

Everything remained quiet in the cabin. Faby looked up again. The man was kneeling beside the terrorist and showing him how to cope with an unconscious person.

Gaby Dillmann came and held the old woman's head. She came to and said: 'Now I want to go to bed and sleep.'

'This is your bed for today, Granny,' Gaby replied, 'My lap is your pillow.'

The old lady complained: 'But I can only sleep on my stomach.'

'Not today,' said Gaby, and began to hum a tune and rock the old lady's head. She was soon asleep.

The small man stayed squatting beside Gaby. He picked up his pistol again. Gaby asked him: 'Do you think all this is necessary?'

'Yes, it is,' he replied.

'I am a pacifist,' said Gaby, 'I don't believe that it can be good for men to fight and kill each other. Could *you* kill somebody?'

'A few months ago I was fighting in Lebanon,' said Wabil Harb, 'There I saw many dead bodies – women and babies as well. They had been killed by the Lebanese fascists with the help of the Israelis. I was in the refugee camp, Tel Zartar, when they reduced it to rubble. For the last 30 years, most of the Palestinians have lived in camps. Should we allow them all to be murdered?'

'War is unlucky for everyone.'

'We must fight and perhaps die to bring peace and justice.'

A pause.

Gaby said, 'Don't you believe that it would be better for both of us if you were in bed with your girlfriend and I was in bed with my boyfriend?'

In the light of the torch Gaby saw that the young man was smiling. She had often thought, 'He's just too good-looking to kill and be killed.'

The young man lifted the pistol to his lips and blew across the top of the barrel, cowboy-fashion. He said nothing more.

For almost half an hour the two of them sat silently together on the floor while the old lady slept.

Meanwhile, Captain Schumann was trying to contact the tower with the last bit of power from the battery. He kept on repeating: 'Send us ground power, send us ground power, send us an emergency power unit.'

Mahmud walked backwards and forwards restlessly. He came across Gaby and said: 'I've got to shoot somebody today. But none of you.' Gaby thought of the journalists

asked how the steps could be lowered without electricity. Schumann explained that there was an emergency release; the steps would fall into place of their own accord.

Mahmud asked: 'And how do you get them up again?'

The pilots guessed that the Palestinian knew more about the technicalities of airplanes than he let on.

Vietor changed tack. 'Perhaps we shouldn't let the steps down,' he said, 'it will be too complicated to get them back up again later. I'll do it a different way.'

The co-pilot let himself down from the forward door on a blanket. Mahmud called after him: 'Don't try to run away. I've got you covered.'

Under the plane, Vietor felt himself suddenly free. It was cooler under there. The cabin and the Palestinian seemed far away. Vietor would have been able to move to the rear under the fuselage without any risk and the hijacker would not have been able to see him. But Vietor immediately dismissed any thought of flight. He could not leave Schumann and the others alone with a mad man who would take his revenge on them. He went over to the emergency unit.

Out on the runway it was very dark and still. There were no lights, except a few from the buildings on which the journalists were encamped and from the distant airport complex. Again, he had to battle against the temptation to run away. He said under his breath: 'It's all been decided for a long time. Either we all go up or we all escape.'

He climbed on to the emergency unit. After a few vain attempts, he managed to get it into gear and brought it up to the right-hand side of the Landshut. He had thought that he would need help to haul the heavy cable over to the machine – but to his surprise he managed it himself.

Then he noticed that he was nervous and trembling. He didn't know where his torch was and couldn't see to turn the power on. He began to throw switches at random. Then he found his torch again, spotted a set of instructions and began to follow them, point by point.

In the cockpit, Schumann was looking at a dead indicator light with the label 'ground power available'. When it lit up, he only had to throw one other switch and the plane would have power again. Several times Vietor came up to the open door on the left-hand side and asked if there was anything happening. He feared that it might only be a matter of minutes before the fearful heat inside overcame some of the passengers. But Schumann replied each time: 'Nothing.'

Eventually, Vietor gave up. 'Pull me back in,' he said, 'I'm not achieving anything.' The small man let down a blanket. But as soon as Vietor tried to put his weight on the improvised rope it slipped through the terrorist's hands. Mahmud ordered Hartwig Faby and another passenger to help. After several more vain attempts, Vietor managed to swing his legs up into the plane and he was hauled inside.

'Captain,' he told Mahmud, 'I couldn't manage it.'

The commando chief gave him some water and told him to go and lie down.

Schumann was beginning to understand why they were not getting any electricity. To switch the plane on to ground power, a battery connection had to be made, but the battery, which now stood at no more than six volts, instead of its usual 24, simply did not have the power to make the connection. Nor was it strong enough to power the radio.

The captain explained the situation to Mahmud: 'Now things are getting critical. Sunrise isn't far off. When the sun hits us, this place is going to be a mass grave. Then you won't need to blow it up.'

Mahmud sat apathetically in the pilot's seat. Schumann asked him if he could send S.O.S. messages with the torch. He nodded. Schumann began to signal, but there was no reply.

Later Vietor tried the same thing with a battery powered spot light. Vietor, once a naval signal man, flashed: 'S.O.S. We urgently need contact. S.O.S.' For every word he flashed, he asked permission. Mahmud simply nodded without paying much attention.

Shortly before sunrise, a car drove up close enough to be told what was needed. A little later, four men brought a battery. The hijackers paid little attention to them. Vietor was allowed to leave the machine for a second time to help with the attachment of the battery. He hoped that there would be some Germans in the group, but they were Arabs, who only spoke a little broken English.

Minutes before the sun came up on the Dubai wilderness, the Landshut's lights came on and the air-conditioning began again. The passengers once again heard Mahmud's voice over the loudspeakers: 'There is no need to strip off any more. Please get dressed again like civilized people.'

The previous night, unnoticed by anybody in the Landshut, a Lufthansa Boeing 707 had landed at Dubai. One passenger on the flight was West Germany's Minister of State, Hans Jürgen Wischnewski. Among his companions was the psychologist, Wolfgang Salewski, who had been Schmidt's adviser since the kidnapping of Schleyer.

Wischnewski immediately had himself taken to Sheik Mohammed, who greeted him warmly: 'You are my guests. You can move about freely here. My men will fulfil every possible wish.' He asked Wischnewski whether he had brought any news from Bonn. No, Wischnewski told him. The Federal Government was not prepared to release arrested terrorists and was seeking for another way to free the hostages.

Wischnewski had been told by Schmidt to ask for permission to send in a select group of commandos, the highly trained *Grenzschutzgruppe-9*, the equivalent of Britain's S.A.S., which had trained for five years in anti-terrorist activities.

The Sheik stalled. 'Everything that happens here will be done by us,' he said, 'I am delegated by my father to make all the decisions. If military action is necessary, my soldiers will undertake it. Be sure that I will do everything to free the hostages.' Wischnewski, impressed, assured the Sheik that he had the full trust of the Federal Government.

The psychologist, Wolfgang Salewski, however, thought the hijackers had been badly handled. 'In every previous hijacking which has ended without bloodshed,' he explained, 'the terrorists have been drawn into negotiation and something has been offered them. Mahmud has been repeatedly told by Sheik Mohammed that he should free the hostages, at least the women and children. Nothing has been offered to him in return. The terrorist must see himself as hemmed in, threatened. In his vacillating psychological state, that's risky.'

Salewski asked to be allowed to speak to the hijacker.

'In accordance with my father's wishes,' replied the Sheik, 'I am responsible for any negotiations.'

Salewski insisted. Under his direction, the Schleyer kidnappers had not so far resorted to murder. He thought he was capable of talking to Mahmud as well. He explained to the Sheik his stragey of defusing the hijackers' aggressions by establishing permanent contact.

Sheik Mohammed listened carefully. Then he said, 'I speak the language of the hijackers and I believe an Arab can understand their mentality better than a European.'

That Sunday morning, the mood on board the Landshut was almost cheerful. The temperature was bearable once again. A catering truck brought breakfast. Many hostages found that, for the first time since their capture, they had a good appetite and they ate heartily.

The Norwegian stewardess, Anna-Maria Staringer, had let slip to her colleagues that it was her 28th birthday that day. Anna-Maria's eyes seemed to betray a feeling of desperation. It seemed as if she had not yet come to terms with the shock of the hijacking. She did not talk much. When she went through the cabin it looked as if she needed all her will to move at all. Yet she helped in silence whenever she was needed.

Mahmud came up as the other members of the crew were congratulating Anna-Maria. He shook her hand and said: 'Well, we ought to have a little party.'

Jürgen Schumann suggested: 'Couldn't we try to get them to bring over a birthday cake and some champagne? It would make a break.'

Mahmud liked the idea. He placed his order with the tower and Sheik Mohammed promised prompt service.

Mahmud went into the cockpit and sat down in the observer's seat. Just across from him, Jürgen Vietor was resting in the co-pilot's seat. They exchanged a few trivialities. Vietor turned half round and put his arm along the back of his chair. He noticed that the Palestinian was staring at his wrist, his face gradually contorting into a rigid.

threatening expression.

Vietor scarcely had time to ask himself, 'Is he going to flip just because the cake is taking too long for him?' when Mahmud screamed: 'What's your religion?' His voice was trembling in a way which signalled one of his sadistic outbursts.

Vietor remembered the threat made in Bahrain that he would be shot on the smallest pretext. The co-pilot was about to say that he was a Protestant ('*Evangelisch*') but he could not think of the right English word.

He stuttered: 'Evangelic,' and immediately knew that the Palestinian would not understand it.

Mahmud shouted: 'What is Evangelic?'

Schumann explained: 'Evangelic lutheric.'

Mahmud had turned purple with rage. He screamed: 'What, what, what?'

In the entrance to the cockpit, Vietor saw the horrified faces of two of the stewardesses. He called out: 'Quickly, what is *Evangelisch* in English?' They said 'Protestant'. Vietor repeated the word.

'You're a liar,' shouted Mahmud, 'You are Jewish. A Zionist.'

'No, certainly not, Captain.'

'Look at your watch! What sort of a watch is that?'

'Its a Junghans.'

'And that?' Mahmud pointed to the trade-mark, a stylized cog-wheel on the watch-face. 'That is a Jewish watch!'

Before they landed in Dubai, Mahmud had ordered all the hostages to give up anything with a Jewish symbol on it and threatened that anyone found later to have 'Zionist goods' on them would be shot immediately. Mahmud put the pistol to the co-pilot's head and screamed in his cracking voice: 'Now I am going to kill you! This is your second mistake! Now you are going to be executed!'

He ordered Vietor into the economy section and pushed him into a free seat. Then he moved through the aircraft with the watch, standing in front of a number of passengers and asking each one: 'Is this a Jewish watch?' The more courageous ones shook their heads. The others shrugged their shoulders.

Vietor was made to place himself between the first-class and economy sections with his hands raised. Schumann talked to Mahmud in incoherent phrases, appealing to his reason and sympathy. Vietor wept, screamed, whimpered, begged for his life.

Mahmud lifted the pistol to the co-pilot's head.

Schumann called out: 'Don't do it, Captain!'

Mahmud suddenly asked gently: 'Didn't you know that this is a Jewish sign?'

At that moment, Vietor lost all hope. Suddenly he felt calm. In a firm, strong voice, he said: 'No, I really didn't, Captain Mahmud.'

The Palestinian let his pistol fall. He threw the watch on the ground and ordered: 'Smash this Zionist thing!'

Vietor stamped on the watch, trying to break it with his heel. He thought: 'It's either it or you,' and jumped on the casing with both feet. But on the soft carpet he did not manage even to break the glass.

Mahmud fetched from the cockpit the hatchet that was for use in case of a crash. He put the watch on an armrest and hit it. It shattered. He handed Vietor the frame which was still attached to the strap: 'Here,' he said, 'a souvenir for you.'

A little later, six champagne bottles arrived at the forward door, along with the cake. It was a nut and cream cake with 28 candles. On it was written in icing sugar: 'Anna-Maria. Happy Birthday'.

Crew members and hijackers surrounded Anna-Maria Staringer in the first-class compartment and wished her well yet again. The stewardesses uncorked the champagne carefully so as not to frighten the passengers. Gaby Dillmann lit the candles. As she did so, she found herself crying and burnt one of her fingers.

Mahmud put on a little show. He postured in front of the curtain dividing the two compartments and announced to the passengers, who had no idea of what was going on, 'We are celebrating today the 28th birthday of our air hostess, Anna-Maria.'

Then he pulled back the curtain to reveal the stewardess who was holding the cake. Anna-Maria Staringer blew out the candles. The passengers clapped and some cheered. For a few moments it sounded like a real party. Mahmud said that everyone was invited to the birthday, except Vietor. Gaby cut the cake into tiny squares and served it up on white napkins. First the children, then the women. All the grown-ups, except Vietor, got a sip of champagne. Everyone waited with their drinks until Mahmud raised his plastic cup and said: 'Anna-Maria: your health.'

People laughed at Vietor and drank toasts to him. He scarcely noticed. Eventually, one of the passengers brought a cup of champagne to him. Vietor declined: 'I am not allowed to,' he said. 'Of course you are,' the man replied, 'Captain Mahmud told me to give it to you.' Vietor took the champagne and swallowed it down.

Meanwhile, the deadline of 8.00 a.m. GMT (11.00 a.m. local time) announced through Payot's office two days before had passed, apparently unremarked by Mahmud.

While the birthday party was under way in the Landshut, another German plane landed at Dubai Airport. It was a two-engined Hawker Siddley belonging to the Brunswick-based Federal Institution for Flight Safety. Out of it climbed GSG-9's commander, Ulrich Wegener, with a small crew of security experts. He had had to leave the rest of his team behind in Ankara. The international news agencies were already sending reports about the 'German specialists' who were following the hijacked Landshut and Wischnewski had had some trouble that morning convincing Sheik Mohammed that Bonn was not planning a second Entebbe.

Wegener met Wischnewski in the VIP lounge. .The minister murmured to the police director: 'For God's sake, don't tell the Arabs who you are. I have a terrific contact with Sheik Mohammed. He is very friendly. But one thing is certain: they see what's happening here as an Arab problem, to be solved by Arabs.'

Wegener had already considered the possibility of storming the Landshut. He thought it could work. Behind the plane were sand dunes which would act as cover.

Then he went with his team into the Dubai Inter-continental. In his room, the German Embassy had put some cold champagne. Outside, it was 100°F in the shade. But

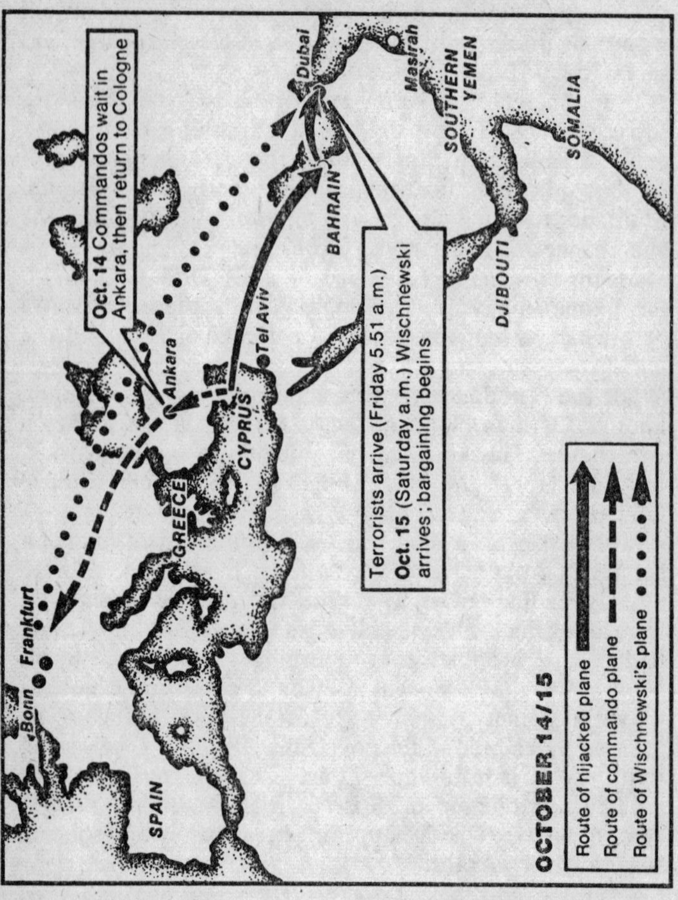

Oct. 14 Commandos wait in Ankara, then return to Cologne
Dubai
Masirah
SOUTHERN YEMEN
SOMALIA
BAHRAIN
Terrorists arrive (Friday 5.51 a.m.)
Oct. 15 (Saturday a.m.) Wischnewski arrives; bargaining begins
DJIBOUTI
Tel Aviv
Ankara
CYPRUS
GREECE
Frankfurt
Bonn
SPAIN
OCTOBER 14/15
Route of hijacked plane
Route of commando plane
Route of Wischnewski's plane

there was no shade. Wegener took a long draught from the bottle. It was approaching 1.00 p.m., just the time at which the hostages got their mouthful of champagne.

Wegener had a shower. Then he washed his socks – he had only brought one spare pair with him.

Back in the airport he met two old acquaintances from England, Major Alistair Morrison and Sergeant Barry Davies. Those, anyway, were the names by which they called themselves outside their barracks in Herefordshire. Morrison and Davies belonged to the SAS, the crack air-force regiment formed during the Second World War to carry out sabotage behind enemy lines. It is now more of an anti-terror unit, with a wealth of experience in Northern Ireland.

Morrison and Davies had visited Wegener three weeks before in Hangelaar. They had taken the opportunity to show him a novelty in their arsenal – a magnesium-filled grenade which exploded with such a bright light and so loud a noise that an unprepared opponent could be incapacitated for at least six seconds by it.

Wegener said he hoped he could use the device against the Schleyer kidnappers. But his British colleagues told him that the grenade was particularly intended for the initial stages of an attack on a hijacked aircraft.

Morrison and Davies had presented themselves in Dubai as agents of the British government, which was, they said, concerned about some of those aboard the Landshut. In fact, they were on loan to GSG-9 from the British government, following a telephone call from Callaghan to Schmidt, in which Callaghan had promised help as a symbol of the international nature of the fight against terrorism.

For Ulrich Wegener, his new colleagues had a very practical value. They had a good deal of excess baggage. In their bags was a collection of their new hardware; and besides, the German could also use the influence of the Englishmen on Dubai's military authorities, who had been trained by the British.

While Wegener was discussing with his colleagues the chances of an assault, Wischnewski came over to the group. He brought bad news. 'The decision is taken,' he said, 'they want to do it themselves. We are not to be involved. The Sheik wants to use his British-trained parachute troops.'

Morrison said: 'They can't do that. They have never practised anything of the kind.'

'In that case we had better start practising immediately,' said Wegener, 'In any event, the plane has got to be recaptured here.'

Wischnewski added, 'The Chancellor too would prefer matters to be settled here. I will do what I can.'

The hostages in the Landshut had a relatively peaceful night. Once again Mahmud did not sleep a wink. Every hour, on the hour, he put his pocket-radio out of the cockpit window and listened to the news on Arabic radio stations. There were reports of an interview between Sheik Mohammed and a journalist. The Sheik had praised Captain Schumann to the skies; he was a marvellous man, the Sheik said, who had smuggled out important information with incredible skill.

After one such broadcast, the Palestinian worked himself into a rage. He threatened Schumann and said that if there were any hostages shot in the morning, the captain would be the first to go.

By dawn however he had calmed down. He ordered the women to take off their shoes and stockings. The stewardesses had to gather them together.

Then he explained over the radio to the tower: 'The plane will have to be refuelled before 9.00 a.m. If it isn't, I'm going to start shooting. First to go will be a 19-year-old, then a 23-year-old, then ten more people at five minute intervals.' Mahmud went into the cabin and made the same announcement.

Gaby Dillmann who had been in a short, deep sleep was woken by Mahmud's voice. She did not understand when Mahmud pointed to a 19-year-old Dutch girl and a young Dutchman: 'You're the first two. Your numbers are 001 and 01.' Then he pointed to Gaby: 'You're number 1.' Then at random he picked out other victims: '2, 3, 4, 5. . . .'

Gaby Dillmann had the feeling that there was ice-cold water running down her back. Then something seemed to explode inside her stomach. She thought: 'I want to get married. I want to marry Rüdeger. I want to have children. I want to have lots of children.'

The woman beside her, Lilo Cramer, tried to comfort her. She asked for her make-up. Gaby gave her back the little bag.

Schumann and Vietor stared towards the airport buildings. But nothing moved. It was ten minutes to nine. The German girl and the Dutchman had to kneel down in the gangway between the first class and economy sections. Mahmud sat in the cockpit, microphone in hand, and watched the second hand of the clock. As every minute passed, he pressed the loud speaker button: 'Another nine minutes ... another eight minutes ... another seven minutes.'

Then Schumann called out: 'Captain! There's a truck coming!' It was a fuel tanker.

Sheik Mohammed's voice came over the radio: 'Would you like some breakfast?'

Mahmud replied promptly: 'That's a good idea. And bring us some more Kleenex as well.'

But nobody fancied any breakfast. Conditions on board were becoming grimmer and grimmer. The 737, which was only designed for short-haul flights, had only two toilets. Both were blocked and only barely usable. A sewage truck arrived. Vietor prodded about in the pans with coat hangers – all in vain. The stink in the cabin was overpowering.

Most of the young women had begun their periods, some because of the excitement, some because their pills were in their hand luggage which the terrorists had gathered up. There were no tampaxes or sanitary towels on board and their clothes were soaked with blood.

Mahmud ordered the passengers to eat. He asked Gaby Dillmann whether Schumann had eaten his food. The pilot had handed back his plate untouched. Gaby was happy to pass on Mahmud's order that he should eat. Schumann should keep up his strength, she said.

That morning the GSG-9 leader, Ulrich Wegener, met Sheik Mohammed in the tower. Wischnewski had described him as a 'German security expert'. Wegener introduced himself only as a colonel, a rank he thought exalted enough for talking to a Sheik. The German told Mohammed a little bit about the techniques of breaking down aircraft doors. The Sheik agreed that his paratroops should be given a rapid introduction to such techniques: 'I would be very grateful to you, if you would support us.'

Wegener ordered some ladders. Then he went over to the airforce base, some two miles from the tower and invisible from the Landshut. There stood a Gulf Air 737 used for training. Twenty Arab soldiers were waiting with English instructors.

Wegener swung himself up on to a wing. Within seconds he had forced in the emergency exit. The surface of the plane had already become so hot in the sun that he burnt his hands. He repeated the exhausting task a few times before he let Mohammed's paratroops have a go. Then he showed them how to break open the front and rear doors.

Twice he made them practice creeping up to the plane, putting ladders in position, opening the doors and storming in. It seemed to go very well. Wegener told the British officers: 'They're not perfect, but they'll do.'

Wegener drove back to the tower in a jeep. Time was pressing. In one hour, the ultimatum set by Schleyer's kidnappers and the 'Martyr Halimeh Commando' was due to expire.

Back in the command post, Wegener saw from the faces of Wischnewski and Mohammed that there was bad news.

'They've refuelled,' said Wischnewski. 'It looks like they are going to take off.' The Sheik had already spoken with his father on the telephone. He was pale and seemed excited. The Germans learned that Dubai's ruler, Sheik Rashid, had told his son to let the plane go.

Sheik Mohammed took the microphone and asked to speak to Mahmud. He appealed to the Palestinian: 'In the name of the President of the United Arab Emirates, Sheik Sajed, and in the name of all the inhabitants of the United Arab Emirates, I beg you to let free all the hostages – or at least the women, the children and the sick.'

'We thank all the representatives of the Government of the United Arab Emirates for their cooperation,' replied

Mahmud. 'We deeply regret that we must reject your request. We have no instructions from our headquarters to comply with them. We've tried to contact our headquarters, but I haven't heard from them.'

Mohammed replied: 'We have tried to reach your headquarters, but without success. In the name of God, the Compassionate, and in the name of all mankind, at least let the children go.'

'The German and Turkish authorities must first let our friends out of prison.'

'That's not in our power,' answered Mohammed.

'So how can you expect me to let the hostages go?'

Mohammed had acted in direct opposition to Salewski's advice. Salewski wanted to reduce tension on board. Sheik Mohammed's aim was that 'they must never be allowed any peace. They mustn't sleep for a minute. We have to keep them busy with something at all times and keep them in a state of tension.'

Now his father's call had put an end to his plans. The Sheik shrugged his shoulders and said: 'I've done everything in my power.' Suddenly it became obvious that he had not slept for two nights. But he immediately took responsibility for his father's decision. 'Had there been any of my countrymen or even Arabs on board, I would have risked anything. But there are only foreigners in the plane. I would be responsible if any of them were killed. That is a responsibility that I cannot bear.'

Wegener, still bathed in sweat, did not quite grasp the situation: 'This shouldn't be allowed,' he said. 'The runways should be blocked. Get the tanks out.'

Wischnewski pointed out of the windows: 'You see the cloud of dust? They're leaving now.' Sand was swirling behind the Landshut. Its engines were running.

'What are we going to do?' said Wegener. 'Where do they want to go?'

At 12.19 p.m. Vietor took off. Mahmud told him to head for Oman. He flew straight ahead and then banked the plane into a left hand curve. Schumann worked out the best height

– 25,000 feet – for the 250-mile flight. He received clearance. It all seemed very routine.

Oman radio was working normally and Schumann raised the tower. Mahmud took over the microphone and said: 'Hello, Hello, we're landing.' He repeated the phrase time after time in a light-hearted tone. The reply was short and to the point: 'You are refused landing permission. The airport is blocked.'

Mahmud told Vietor at the controls: 'Okay then: to Aden.' Schumann worked out the distance and estimated their fuel requirements: 'We may just do it,' he said. He asked for and received permission to move up to 33,000 feet, the altitude he considered most economical. Vietor set the plane on course for Aden.

As they were on their way south the two pilots had a slight disagreement. Schumann wanted to fly direct over an 'air defence identification zone' which was a military area closed to civil aircraft. 'Nobody will do anything to us,' he said. 'They know who we are.'

Vietor disagreed: 'If we go over there, they'll shoot us down. It will only cost us a few miles more to fly round.' Schumann eventually agreed. Mahmud sat silently in the observer's seat.

In the desert, they saw a runway not marked on their maps. 'Captain Mahmud,' asked Schumann, 'Shouldn't we go down here? We're soon going to be damn low on juice.'

Mahmud hesitated for a few seconds and then announced: 'We're going on to Aden.'

ADEN

Mahmud's lethargy dropped from him and he began to shift about nervously again.

He called Hind Alameh into the cockpit and gave her an order. The girl began to tie up the passengers with the stockings collected in Dubai. The 'young one' fastened explosives to the cabin wall in front of the economy section and lay matches and fuses carefully in the first class section.

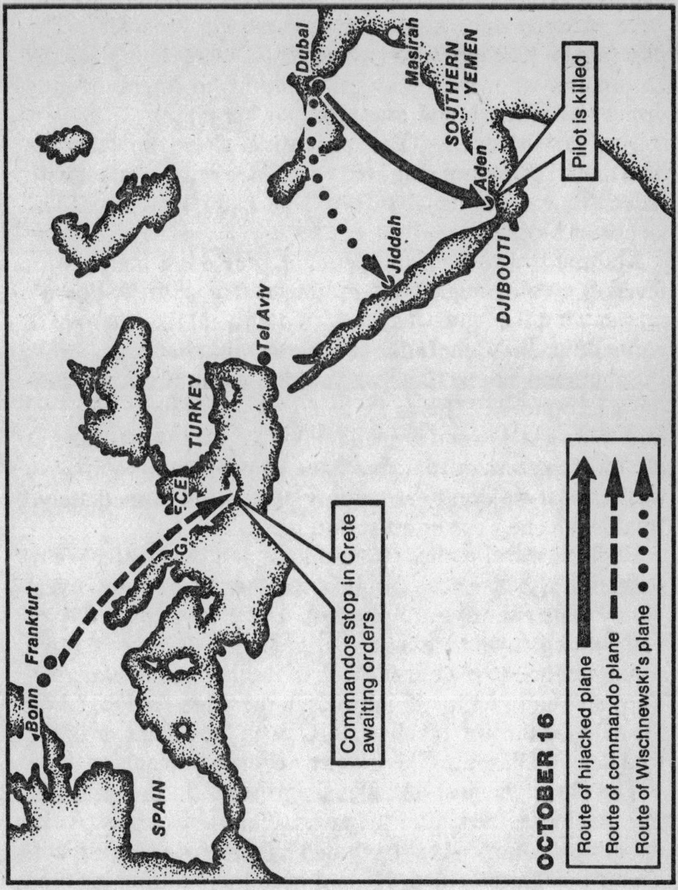

Bonn
Frankfurt
SPAIN
TURKEY
Tel Aviv
Jiddah
DJIBOUTI
Aden
SOUTHERN YEMEN
Masirah
Dubai
Commandos stop in Crete awaiting orders
Pilot is killed
OCTOBER 16
Route of hijacked plane
Route of commando plane
Route of Wischnewski's plane

He fixed the wires behind the tables that were clipped back against the wall.

The hostages had been glad to leave Dubai. They had been afraid of another night without air conditioning and believed things could only get better. Now, suddenly, they were plunged once again into uncertainty and fear. The passengers had no idea where they were going. Gaby Dillmann, who muttered information to them at any opportunity, was not allowed to leave her place.

Navigation was easy. The coast was as clear below them as on a map. Schumann managed to get into radio contact with Aden. It was the usual story: 'You can't land here. The airport is blocked.'

Mahmud, who had not slept for four days, stared with feverish eyes through the windscreen. He said: 'It doesn't matter what they say – it doesn't matter what they do – we're going down in Aden. It doesn't matter what happens.'

Schumann began to speak rapidly, without pauses, into the microphone: 'This is an emergency. We have no more fuel. We must descend immediately if we are going to land at all. Please get an official. We have 90 people on board. We will crash if we don't get landing permission immediately.' By this time he was almost shouting.

Flight Control replied: 'Stand by, stand by, please. We're checking.' After a few minutes, another voice came over: 'Sorry. The runways are blocked. There's no possibility of you coming down here.'

Schumann made a quick check of the flying time available. They still had fuel for 25 minutes in the tank. He looked on the map for the nearest airport. It lay on the other side of the Red Sea, in Djibouti. There was no chance of reaching it.

The plane was just 40 miles from Aden. In the clear air, they could see the end of the peninsular quite clearly. At its tip, almost completely surrounded by water, was the airport. Vietor recognized Aden. He had been there during his time in the Navy, when it had still been under British rule.

A few minutes later, the two men could see two runways in the sand that did not appear on their map, but it was not possible to see what sort of a sub-structure they had.

Vietor went down to 3,000 feet and swept in over the

airport from the east. The sun was already low on the horizon and dazzled them. They could only vaguely make out the obstacles on the runway.

'We've got 700 kilos of fuel,' said Schumann. Fifteen minutes. He read out the ever decreasing amount on the fuel gauge as if he was supervising a count-down.

Vietor swept out over the sea again and approached the airport from the west with the sun behind him. Now they could see that all the hard runways, even the surfaces in front of the airport buildings, had been blocked with armoured cars, and there were still more vehicles driving into position.

Schumann had already announced several times that he had to land. There came no further reply from the tower. The two pilots no longer had any illusions: the vehicles were not going to withdraw at the last moment, as they had at Dubai.

Mahmud gave some instructions in Arabic to his companions in a low, hoarse voice. Schumann told the stewardesses that they should prepare for a crash landing.

The girl hijackers had only bound about half of the passengers. Now they began to undo the knots and cut through the stockings. The hostages helped. The young man rolled up fuses and packed away the explosives in a bag.

The chief stewardess, Hannelore Piegler, looked out the instruction leaflet for emergency landings. She went to the microphone in the front of the cabin and began to read: 'Ladies and Gentlemen. . . .'

Half way through she broke off and began to stow loose objects away in the cabin, as stated in the instructions. From the cockpit, somebody called out that they were about to touch down. Gaby Dillmann seized the microphone that was dangling at the end of its flex. 'Look out everyone . . .' she began.

Hannelore Piegler asked for the microphone. She said that that was her task and asked what Gaby Dillmann thought she was doing. Hannelore Piegler felt she should be responsible for giving the instructions, and that the younger, spontaneous and emotional Gaby was acting against instructions. But Hannelore Piegler was almost at the end of her tether, like almost all the hostages. Gaby Dillmann noticed as much. She had seen how the passengers had hardly reacted at all to the formal and abstract emergency instructions.

She did not give up the microphone. She did not know the instructions off by heart, because in her training she had never concentrated particularly on emergency landings. But she was sure that she knew the essentials. Besides, there was no time to read out the extensive catalogue of items. She began to recite some rules of her own: 'The main thing is to keep calm. You know how good our pilots are. I'm sure everything will go well.' And then she reeled off the most important safety precautions that she could think of: 'Drop everything with a point on it – biros, combs, brushes, jewellery and glasses – and above all false teeth – you might swallow them.'

Anna-Maria Staringer went silently, as if in a dream, along the gangway with a plastic bag. Passengers threw false teeth into the bag, along with jewellery, writing implements. Gaby told them to use everything that remained in the racks to pad out the cabin.

Gaby showed the position to be adopted in an emergency landing: leaning forward, head on knees, hands folded across the nape of the neck, relaxed. She explained: 'Above all don't sit upright when we hit. Keep your heads down because usually there are a number of impacts. If you do as I've described you'll be fine.'

The two girl hijackers had sat down and put on their safety belts. The young man acted the hero. With raised pistol in one hand and hand grenade in the other, he stood in the middle of the gangway. Gaby Dillmann told him forcibly: 'Sit down!' He looked astonished but sat down and put the hand grenade on safety.

According to instructions, the captain should have announced when touchdown was imminent but Gaby guessed that there would be other things on his mind. They were coming in low over the water. She called out: 'Chairs upright! Heads down!'

In the cockpit, Schumann said 'Another 400 kilos' – at most, four to five minutes flying time. Vietor said: 'It's too late now anyway.' The airport was straight in front of them.

Vehicles were still driving on to the runways.

The plane was now at under 500 feet. Vietor put down the flaps, released the undercarriage and began his final approach. He turned to Schumann and said: 'It was a nice life, but a bit short. Oh, well.' He was quite matter of fact. There was no sign of panic, or even fear.

'Well,' replied Schumann, 'it's almost over.' They shook hands.

Vietor turned round to Mahmud. He sat as usual in the observer's seat behind the captain. His eyes were half closed, his mouth open. His face was drained. He looked like a corpse. Sweat was running down his face. He had said nothing for several minutes. He was motionless. The two men could not make out whether he was incapacitated with terror or whether he was simply awaiting the planned end of his mission with resignation.

Vietor put out his hand to him. He shook it: 'Goodbye Captain,' he said, and Mahmud replied: 'Goodbye.'

At that moment Vietor saw that the Palestinian had not got his seat-belt on. He banked the plane sharply and shouted: 'Seat belt!'

'Are you mad?' Schumann shouted, 'We've got no more fuel!'

Vietor shouted back: 'I don't give a shit! He's got to do up his seat belt, otherwise he'll go through the windscreen!'

The co-pilot pulled out of his turn to begin his approach again. At this point he should have been at 50 feet, but the plane was scarcely 30 feet clear of the water. Schumann shouted that they were going down, but Vietor was sure that he could bring the machine up again. As a former marine pilot he was used to flying close to the waves. The plane climbed, and Vietor began to circle again.

Later he could not explain why he had put everyone in the Landshut in danger in order to save Mahmud's life, but as soon as he shook hands with the man who had threatened him with death so many times he no longer seemed an enemy. He became simply one of three men who sat together facing death.

Mahmud fingered the seat-belt. His arms and hands did not seem to belong to him any more. He sat stiffly in his seat.

Schumann tried to get the belt around him but could not manage it. Vietor had to help.

Meanwhile the machine had flown in a full circle. Vietor aimed at a free stretch of sand between the blocked runways. He throttled right back, cut speed, put on the air brakes, and put the flaps down. He saw earth and stones beneath him. Impact. The landing gear did not bury itself in the sand as the pilots had feared. The plane bounced a couple of times. In the cabin, a few blankets fell out.

Vietor threw the brakes on. He called to Schumann: 'Fire extinguishers!' Schumann pulled three red levers. Automatically, the fuel supply, the hydraulics and the electricity were all cut off and fire extinguishers opened in the engines.

The engines were still running. Schumann and Vietor looked at each other. Then suddenly the co-pilot said: 'Shit! We forgot to switch off!' He threw a switch and silence fell.

The three men looked out. Nobody said anything. Vietor threw up his arms as if about to give a shout of joy. He opened the window to see whether everything was all right with the plane and if there was any sign of fire. He looked at the setting sun which seemed to be lying on the edge of the landing ground. Then an impenetrable cloud of dust, whipped up by their landing, blanketed the plane.

The sun turned the dust red. The plane seemed to be bathed in a sea of fire. Vietor slammed the window shut.

The men undid their safety belts. As the dust cleared, they checked that the Landshut had not sustained any visible damage. Mahmud seized Vietor's arm. He said: 'I'll kill myself before I kill you.'

Schumann went back into the cabin. The two girls were holding each other by the hand and talking and laughing together, excited as children. The young man was laughing as well.

Schumann did not say anything as he went down the gangway, smiling. The passengers took his smile to be the 'all clear'. Schumann had never been allowed to speak much to them, but his appearance – calm and self-confident – gave the passengers a feeling of security.

Mahmud announced that Vietor had been the pilot. The passengers clapped, called 'bravo' and a few cheered. Jürgen

Vietor took the stewardesses' microphone and said: 'Well, it wasn't a crash landing. We are still alive.' The passengers clapped again.

Outside in the gathering gloom several hundred soldiers were running towards the plane. A hundred yards away they formed a circle with their weapons raised. Behind, a second and then a third cordon formed. Armoured cars drove out.

The stewardesses opened the doors. Vietor took the loud-hailer and shouted: 'Don't shoot! We are peaceful people! This is a German aeroplane. We had to make an emergency landing. We would like to speak to a German representative, please.'

He went to all three doors and made the same announcement. The soldiers stood silently, covering the plane with their weapons.

Schumann meanwhile was trying to establish radio contact with the tower. Nobody replied.

Vietor shouted in English: 'Send us a government official! We have to speak to somebody!'

Mahmud took the loud-hailer and began to talk in Arabic to the soldiers, who were now mere silhouettes in the twilight. The whole airport seemed ominously quiet. The only sound was that of the plane's auxiliary turbine.

Gaby Dillmann fetched from the toilet the bag of objects collected before the landing. She held them up one at a time, gave a short description and handed them out to the owners. There was a bit of confusion over the false teeth, to the considerable amusement of those who still had their own teeth.

The stewardesses gave out water. Vietor picked up a luggage-rack flap which had been jerked off in the landing and took it to the rear door. He threw it out into the darkness: 'Don't shoot! I'm only throwing something out of the plane which was broken off. It's quite harmless.'

The cover fell on to stones with a clatter. Vietor ducked back under cover. Outside, everything remained quiet.

After half an hour or so there came a voice in Arabic through a loud-hailer. Mahmud replied. There followed a discussion, which became increasingly heated, between the hijacker and the man who stood unseen out in the darkness.

When silence fell again, Mahmud said to the pilots: 'There's nothing we can do. We have to leave again.'

Schumann and Vietor, speaking together and interrupting each other, replied: 'That's complete madness ... after an emergency like that you can't possibly start up again ... the landing gear is bound to have suffered ... the engines are full of sand ... we've got no more fire extinguishers if we have another emergency.'

Mahmud shouted angrily out into the night. He repeated in Arabic the many reasons why it was impossible to take off again. He knew enough about aeroplane technology to take them seriously. Some people came up to the Landshut who said they were mechanics. They had a look around the machine. One said in bad English: 'Everything okay. We see nothing wrong. You can start.'

Schumann and Vietor did not believe him. Schumann said to Mahmud: 'We can't rely on them. I must have a look outside. I've got to get down and see for myself.' Mahmud nodded.

Since the emergency landing, the relationship between the kidnappers and the crew had changed. They talked together as partners. It was clear from a number of small gestures and references that Mahmud was grateful for Vietor's warning to put on his seat-belt before the emergency. At that point, the situation had been reversed. It was the pilots who exercised authority over life or death. Together they had prepared to die and now, together, they were alive. Outside were hostile Yemenis who clearly made no distinction between hostages and kidnappers. The Palestinians, having risked their necks to land in what they thought was a friendly country, clearly felt betrayed.

So Mahmud unhesitatingly gave Schumann permission to leave the aircraft. Schumann dropped to the ground. He took out a torch and went around the aeroplane. After a few minutes he called up: 'The landing gear still looks okay. There's nothing bent that I can see. Can't see any damage of any kind.' He was speaking in German now. The pilots had ignored Mahmud's orders only to speak in English since the emergency landing. Mahmud made no objections.

Vietor and Mahmud sat next to each other in the forward

doorway. Their bodies were touching. They let their legs knock against each other. Now and then Schumann ducked across to the other side as he checked the machine.

Then the two men did not see him for several minutes. Vietor thought he might have found some damage. Mahmud remained calm. But when he suddenly jumped up and leaned out of the door in order to see the captain Vietor shouted: 'Jürgen, where are you? What's happening?' There was no reply.

Mahmud's expression changed again. He ran into the cockpit and seized the microphone. Shortly before, he had been in contact with the tower. Now he shouted, his voice cracking. There was a reply in Arabic. Mahmud turned to Vietor: 'I've told the Yemenis that if the pilot doesn't come back, I'm going to blow up the plane. They've promised to shoot him if they find him and he doesn't return to the plane of his own accord.'

Vietor wondered why Schumann had vanished. One possibility was that he had lost his head and simply run away. But Schumann had as much nerve as his co-pilot. Vietor assumed that if he had run away he would be hoping to make contact with a Yemeni official with a view to finding a German representative, in the belief that a take-off after an emergency landing would be too great a risk.

Vietor went to Gaby Dillmann: 'Schumann's beaten it,' he whispered to Gaby. Gaby had dozed off. Now she started up: 'Has he gone mad?' she asked. Then her old optimism returned: 'He's trying to get in contact with Germans,' she said, 'and get something done at last.'

Vietor was more pessimistic: 'Jürgen's going to be shot, either by the Yemenis or Mahmud.' He took Mahmud's threat seriously. He picked up the megaphone and called through each of the three opened doors in turn: 'Jürgen where are you? Come back! The Yeminis are going to shoot you!' He repeated it in German and in English. He called a fourth time through the cockpit window. But outside everything remained still.

The passengers had not yet properly realized that Schumann had gone. For many of them, nothing seemed to be real any more, just a bad dream, or a fairy tale in which they found themselves unwittingly embroiled.

Certainly the scene through the windows had an air of unreality. Weak moonlight turned sand and stones snow white. Some asked the stewardesses where they were. How could it be so hot and so snowy at the same time? Were they in Greenland, perhaps?

Mahmud's voice cut through the dreams. He picked up the megaphone and shouted out in Arabic. Then he explained to the hostages in English: 'If the pilot doesn't come back, I am going to blow up the plane. If he comes back, I am going to execute him. Those are the two possibilities.'

Vietor sat for a few minutes in the open door, cooling himself in the breeze. Then Mahmud called him into the cabin. Vietor felt that the Palestinian, uncontrolled and raving as he was, still had some respect for him. With a wave of his hand, which somehow seemed apologetic, Mahmud told the co-pilot to sit with the passengers.

Everyone on board had lost all feeling of time. Vietor thought that they had been waiting for almost an hour. Gaby Dillmann thought that it had been longer. Then Mahmud calmly announced: 'The authorities have at last captured the pilot. They are going to hand him over to us for execution. He has betrayed me. He set his lousy life against yours. That's why he's going to die.'

Gaby Dillmann translated, adding at the end: 'We can only all hope that the worst won't come to the worst.'

Then she went back to her place in the third row and put her safety belt on. At first, she still had hope. Although Mahmud acted evil, she thought to herself, he must be pleased that Schumann was trying to establish contact with the Germans. He would surely agree that Bonn must be told how serious the situation was.

But she became cold and panicky. She had established a personal contact with Schumann. Both had memories of the same town, the same school, the same teachers. She feared for him. The more she thought, the more her hopes for Schumann slipped away. She pulled a blanket over her head as if to escape her own thoughts. She practically abandoned hope for Schumann. Subconsciously, she knew that

Mahmud's tone was different than in his previous exhibitionist displays of sadism. Eventually, the most she dared hope was that Mahmud would shoot him at the back, away from the children.

Hartwig Faby, who always tried to analyse things as objectively as possible, noticed contradictory feelings in himself – on the one hand, fear of what might happen to Schumann, on the other the possibility that the pilot might have fled the group that was still forced to obey the terrorists, and in so doing had threatened them all. There seemed a justification for Mahmud's anger.

Mahmud looked out of the forward door on to the dark airfield. He called: 'There he comes! Now I'm going to hold a revolutionary trial.' He ordered Hannelore Piegler to let down the rear steps.

Schumann stood alone beside the plane. A 100 yards behind him, in the shadows, stood soldiers. Schumann came up the steps. He looked blankly in front of him. Without hesitation he went along the gangway up to Mahmud who stood in the entrance to the first class section.

For a few seconds the two men looked each other in the eye. Then Mahmud shouted: 'Down on your knees!'

Behind Mahmud were the three other terrorists. The 'small one' had put something over her shoulders, despite the heat. She sat on the seat and ate an apple. The 'fat one' had put on some glasses. All three smiled their stony, withdrawn smiles.

Schumann knelt with his hands folded over his head. Mahmud put his right foot on an empty seat and said: 'This is a revolutionary tribunal. You have put us all in danger of being blown up. You have already betrayed me once before. I cannot forgive you a second time. Are you guilty? Or are you not guilty?'

'Captain,' replied Schumann in a low, quiet voice, 'there were difficulties about getting back to the plane.'

Mahmud hit him in the face with his left hand, still holding the pistol with his right hand. He screamed: 'Guilty or not guilty?'

Schumann never even begged for his life; he said: 'Excuse me, sir, may I explain. . . . There were difficulties. . . .'

Mahmud hit him in the face again: 'Are you guilty?'

'You . . . you won't let me explain. I couldn't get back to the plane.'

Mahmud hit Schumann so hard that his head rocked. Then he shot him in the face. Schumann fell.

After the shot, the only noise in the cabin was the humming of the power unit. The 'fat one' screamed: 'Anyone who speaks or cries will be shot immediately.'

Mahmud lit a cigarette. Then there came a child's voice, very loud in the silence. It was Steffen Waida, whose third birthday it was that day. He was sitting just beside Schumann's body. He said: 'Daddy, it went bang.'

Hartwig Faby had been able to see only Mahmud's face over the back of the seat in front of him. It had suddenly distorted, then came the report. Faby thought, 'That wasn't a real shot.' The only ones he had heard before had been in the cinema or on television. This seemed somehow drier, louder, with no echo. Faby thought Mahmud might have used a blank. But at the same time through his left foot, which was in the gangway, he felt the vibration of Schumann's body hitting the floor. When it lay quite still and Mahmud turned away with a cigarette in his lips, Faby knew that the shot had been real.

He remained very calm, as all the passengers did. His first thoughts were entirely selfish: 'Now they'll throw the body out of the plane, then the whole world will know that the hijackers are serious. The government will have to give in at last, immediately. They cannot risk the death of other people.'

Only a few of the hostages wept. Gaby, her head still under the Lufthansa blanket, glanced fearfully out from underneath. She saw Schumann's feet near her. She sobbed out loud. The 'fat one' screamed at her, and threatened to shoot. Gaby hardly heard her. It was dark round about her, but she saw Schumann's face in front of her. First it seemed to be Schumann alive, then it became unclear, then it became a distorted vision, blood-smeared, with open mouth and staring eyes.

Lilo Cramer put an arm around her. Someone behind tried to stroke her. She took the blanket from her head, but did not dare to open her eyes for fear of seeing the dead man. Somebody put a glass of water into her hand. She held it firm. She tried hard to think of the glass in her hand. She drank, and concentrated on the water in her mouth, then on the water as it went down her throat. Then she thought of Steffen and his 'Daddy, it went bang.'

That helped. She found she could control her weeping. She whispered to Lilo Cramer: 'Where's he lying?'

'They've put a blanket over him,' she replied. Gaby opened her eyes.

Mahmud called from the first class section that the 'air-hostess' should come and translate. He could only mean Gaby. She did not move.

Behind her Hannelore Piegler stood up. In the narrow gangway it was scarcely possible to get past Schumann's body without touching it. She supported herself with her hands on the arm-rests on either side and eased herself slowly over the body.

Three of the terrorists were in the cockpit. There was loud laughter. The 'fat one' stood with a pistol in front of the passengers. In the cabin it was deathly still, suddenly the old man began to talk loudly. First, he balanced a glass of water on the head of the woman in front of him and laughed. Then he began: 'Now I want to go home. I have an important engagement. We've been here too long. I'm getting out now.' His wife backed him up. She repeated sentences she had said many times before: 'I have to go as well. I have to be at the hairdresser at six. I can't be late.' She began to comb her hair with a plastic fork.

The old man stood up. All the terrorists ignored the two old people. But the passengers became unsettled. Despite the ban on speaking, there were some excited whispers, then voices. Somebody shouted: 'Shut up!' Another voice said: 'Someone hit him on the chin!'

Accumulated hate, fear and aggression poured out at the crazy old man, who had been laughed at often enough and whose mutterings had often seemed the only sane thing about the recent events.

Faby also felt this mixture of anger and fear. But above all he feared that the loud excited voices would bring Mahmud out of the cockpit again. He made signs to Sayeh that he would look after the old man. She nodded. Faby undid his seat belt and went up to the old fellow who was standing beside his seat. The teacher hit him hard enough in the chest to make him tumble back into his seat. The old man remained silent after that.

Gaby thought about Schumann. She thought of him as a hero. He had intervened when the Palestinian threatened to shoot Vietor and the three alleged Jews. He had risked his life to get out information. When Mahmud discovered, and accused him of 'betrayal', Schumann did not deny it, and never lost his self-control.

Since then Gaby had seen the hate in Mahmud's eyes when he looked at the captain. Schumann had had to sit alone in the cabin for a long time without talking to anyone. He must have known that he would be the first victim. Perhaps that had contributed to his decision not to return to the machine. Twice he had helped to save Vietor's life and he had intervened whenever a passenger was threatened, yet when he was killed no one had dared stand up or say a word.

Suddenly, the lights and air-conditioning died. The last litre of fuel was used up. Vietor was told to go into the cockpit. He stood up. There were no emergency lights either. Vietor knew that he would tread on Schumann's body in the dark. He shouted out: 'Put a torch on! I can't get over otherwise!'

There was no torch and Vietor had to feel his way over the body. In the cockpit, he switched off everything but some emergency lighting which ran off the battery. He knew from Dubai that nothing would work if the battery was used up. He sat down with the hijackers, who made a few tense jokes and laughed. Vietor laughed with them. Mahmud seemed friendly again.

Then Vietor was allowed to sit alone in the open door again. Outside, a Yemeni officer came up. 'You have to leave as soon as possible,' he said. 'We will give you technical assistance. But as soon as you get clearance, you have to leave.'

The Yemenis had reason for haste. They were awaiting the East German Defence Minister who was expected to offer military aid and the government wanted to avoid having the hijacked machine at the airport when he arrived.

But Vietor wanted to delay the start until the morning. With a possibly defective machine, a night take-off would be suicide. He began to plan delaying tactics. He ordered only 200 gallons of fuel for each tank so that the plane would remain light when he tried to get it out of the sand. The tanker got stuck in the sand. It took a few minutes to get it clear. Then Vietor said that refuelling under pressure was not possible because the plane had no power. There would have been enough power in the battery, but the Yemenis fell for the trick. It took them some time to find a hose, and prepare to refuel on the wing. The hose proved too short and the Yemenis had to look for a longer one.

In the cabin, meanwhile, it was becoming unbearably hot, but the doors were open and the hostages could move about. Only Mahmud carried a weapon. The others were friendly and helped anyone who needed help. Harb and Sayeh spoke to the hostages for the first time. Sayeh came over to Gaby, who was still in shock after the murder, and said: 'Captain Martyr Mahmud had to do it. The captain had betrayed him twice and broken his word, but he never felt a thing. I saw it all. Captain Martyr Mahmud hit him. Schumann thought he was only going to get hit. When his head was turned, after the last blow, Captain Martyr Mahmud shot him. He never saw a thing.'

Somehow, Gaby felt comforted. Suddenly she saw Sayeh, who up until then had screamed and threatened continuously, in a new light. She felt a need to talk to her.

Harb got into conversation with the beauty queens. He told them he had wanted to be an engineer. The terrorists always spoke of themselves in the past tense. Whenever death was mentioned, they would say: 'We have been dead a long time.'

Harb spoke a little German to the beauty queens and with Hans Hasse Heyn he talked in French. Heyn asked if the body could not be removed. Harb promised to mention it to Mahmud.

Gaby went forward, over Schumann's body, supporting

herself on the arms of the seats. The carpet was sodden with blood. Gaby was wearing rubber soled shoes taken aboard in Dubai. She felt blood under her feet, and tried not to think of it.

The temperature was now over 120°F. The body was beginning to smell. This, combined with the stink of the toilets, made the air almost unbreathable.

Vietor, nevertheless, was still trying to delay take-off. There were still six hours to go before daylight. When eventually there was fuel in the tanks, Vietor suggested that the baggage be removed to make the machine lighter. Mahmud talked to the Yemenis and then he said there was no question of that. Vietor guessed that it was because they had extra explosive in their cases. 'Then you have to pull us out of here,' Vietor said, 'I hope you have a strong tractor!' They had a tractor, but no tow-bar. Vietor said: 'If you can't pull me out, I'll have to use the engines. But to get the engines going, I need ground power.'

Mahmud had told the soldiers that he wanted to throw a body out of the plane. They had forbidden him to do it. Alameh, Sayeh and Harb put a blanket around the head of Schumann's body and dragged it down the gangway to the rear cupboard. Gaby was told to take out the cases and coats. The terrorists stood the corpse upright in the small space and locked the door. Then they wiped the blood off their hands with paper towels.

The 'small one', Hind Alameh, found a dust-pan and broom. She swept up some brain that was still on the carpet. Then suddenly she became very pale, put down the dust-pan on a first class seat and began to laugh hysterically.

Mahmud took the dust-pan, went to the open cockpit window and threw it out.

Gaby Dillmann stood for a few seconds with trembling hands before the great spot of blood. She pulled herself together. She said to Harb: 'The blood will soon start to go bad. We have to get it away.' Then she retreated, fearing she would be asked to cope with it. But Harb merely poured a bottle of gin over the stain and put a blanket over it.

The Yemenis brought an auxiliary power unit to the plane. It delivered 200 volts. Vietor said: 'I'm sorry. We need

115 volts.'

Eventually the correct unit arrived. Soon he was able to turn on his inboard power unit and with it the air-conditioning and the main lights. The doors were closed.

Vietor told Mahmud that he would have to help him. Mahmud sat in Schumann's place. Vietor told him how to read out the check list. The Palestinian seemed disorganized and left points out. Vietor corrected him – he knew the check list off by heart.

Vietor started the engines. Everything seemed almost in order. The exhaust temperatures were a little too high, but not critical. There must have been a good deal of sand partially blocking the airstream.

He increased power. Then he heard a scream from the cabin. Passengers called out: 'We're burning! There's smoke!' Vietor cut the engines. 'We've no more fire extinguishers,' he said to Mahmud, 'We used them on landing.'

A stewardess came into the cockpit and said; 'False alarm.' The cold blast of the air-conditioning had turned the cabin's damp heat into steam.

Vietor started the engines again. It was still dark in front of the plane. Of the five headlights, only one worked. The others had been damaged on landing. A car lit the sand in front. The co-pilot increased power, but the plane, its tyres sunk deep in the sand, did not move. Then gradually, it began to roll forward.

As indicated by the tower, Vietor brought the plane to the end of the runway. They were being followed by a military convoy which immediately surrounded them again. All three tanks were filled.

There was still two hours to go before dawn. Vietor tried to convince the tower of his problem: 'We can't start at night. . . . We have no headlights. . . . Even if we take off, we can't land anywhere except in daylight. . . . I have no navigational system. . . . The engines are full of sand. . . . I've no idea where the captain wants us to go.'

The tower remained adamant: 'You have to leave immediately!' he was told.

Vietor asked about the weather. The tower wanted to

know for what area. Mahmud would not say. 'We shall be flying about a thousand miles,' Vietor told the tower, 'please give me the weather report on this whole area.'

'We will give you the information in the air. Take off now!'

Vietor was certain that the Yemenis would open fire if he did not obey. He was not sure whether the newly refuelled plane could take off in the space available. The hot weather and the sand in the engines would hinder his acceleration.

His fears were confirmed when he increased power. There were explosions, caused by the reduced airflow.

The tower warned again: 'You have to take off now! This is your last warning!'

Vietor asked once again for a weather report.

'We'll give it to you up there!' came the reply. 'Go now!'

Vietor gave up. It did not even occur to him to tell the passengers to put on their safety jackets in case the plane went down in the sea. He applied the throttle and turned on the auxilliary power unit. Normally the engines powered the air-conditioning, but it cut performance and the Landshut needed all the power it could get.

Mahmud read through the check-list again. Vietor applied full power and trod on the brakes. When everything was stable, Vietor released the brakes. The Landshut rolled forward. Acceleration was poor. The runway lights were switched on and Vietor could see to the end. A hundred yards short of the red lights, behind which loomed the sea, the Landshut rose laboriously. Vietor began to climb.

Suddenly he remembered that Aden was ringed with mountains. He had seen them on landing. He asked the tower: 'Are there mountains in front of me?'

The tower replied drily: 'Your minimum height should be 2,500 feet.'

They were at 2,000 feet. There was no sense in banking. Vietor did not know where the mountains were. He could only try to gain height as quickly as possible. The Landshut climbed slowly to 2,500 feet. Vietor had had no chance to orientate himself, for Aden's radio beacon was not working. Only after a number of requests was it switched on.

At last Mahmud said: 'We're flying to Mogadishu.'

Vietor asked in amazement where that was. The Palestinian showed him the Somali capital on a map in a passenger information folder. Vietor found Mogadishu on a navigational map of South West Asia, far down in the left-hand corner. He had never been down there. The 737 did not fly long stretches.

But he found he could pick up the Djibouti radio bcacon on the Somali border, and he was also getting some support now from the Aden tower. The Yemenis gave him a weather report and information about Mogadishu airport. Vietor transmitted calls on the emergency frequency 121/5 and asked for radar back-up. He did not know that there was no radar in this region. The plane was still climbing very slowly. Vietor took out the technical handbook and correlated weight, outside temperature and engine readings. He concluded that everything was OK. It still bothered him that the fire extinguishers were empty, which meant that if there was a fire the plane would inevitably explode.

Mahmud chain smoked. He was very quiet. He had put his gun away and was attempting to fulfil the function of a co-pilot.

The 737 could, once in the air, be flown by one man. Vietor remembered how, when he was in training on a flight from Turin to Frankfurt, his captain had suddenly said: 'Now I'm dead' and retired behind a newspaper. But now, after the fourth night without sleep, somewhere between Arabia and Africa, without sufficient navigational help, things were not so simple.

They flew over Djibouti. Its radio beacon became weaker and weaker behind them. Vietor found another on the map and tuned in. It was shut down.

He drew a line between Djibouti and Mogadishu and computed a course. There seemed to be a steady west wind. Vietor did some ready reckoning: '156°, a westerly wind of perhaps 40 knots, which could put me five knots out, so I'll steer 160°. It doesn't matter too much; sometime, I'll see the coast again.' The other terrorists came into the cockpit occasionally. They were carrying their hand grenades again and smoking. The safety pins were hanging from their fingers. If they dropped one of the grenades, it would inevitably explode. Things were back to normal.

Vietor picked up the radio beacon at Belet Uen, just over the Somali border. He established that the wind was stronger than he thought and had driven him off course. He banked over the radio beacon to get back on course.

Up ahead, he picked up the Mogadishu beacon.

MOGADISHU

Vietor flew towards the beacon. It was getting light and in a few minutes the sun burst out of the sea. Mahmud pulled down some sun blinds.

Vietor picked up other planes radioing Mogadishu for information. He could have spoken to the Somalis direct but he suggested to Mahmud: 'We'd better not announce ourselves or they'll bar the runway. Perhaps they haven't seen us yet. There doesn't seem to be any radar in this area and no air defence.'

Mahmud nodded. Vietor remained over the water because he did not know if there were any coastal mountains. He went down to 2,000 feet and flew parallel to the coast. They approached Mogadishu. Vietor saw the runway directly on the coast line. It was not blocked. There seemed, at this early hour, to be nothing moving on the airfield at all. An excited, incomprehensible voice was attempting to make contact with them over the radio. He made no reply.

The cabin was made ready for landing. Mahmud read the 'approach' check list. Again in his nervousness he left out a few points. Possibly he did not think that such regulations were important. Vietor made a final circle, let down the landing gear and lowered the flaps. Mahmud, with more concentration this time, read the final check list. Vietor told him to look out for any planes taking off or landing, for they still had made no contact with the tower.

Vietor made a smooth landing. On the airfield, people were running about in total confusion. Eventually, someone came up and waved them in. Mahmud had to work the nose wheel. The steering was extremely delicate: even captains have been known to have difficulty in manoeuvring 737's with precision.

Vietor guided him: 'This way, this way, stop, back a bit, back a bit.' The Landshut moved in a zig-zag over the runway and after two final turns the plane reached its allotted space.

There was no direct contact with the tower. Vietor waved through the open cockpit window at a black who was running excitedly around the plane. The co-pilot asked Mahmud: 'Do they speak English or French here?'

'Perhaps French,' Mahmud guessed.

Vietor tried: *'Parlez vous français?'* The black shook his head, but he seemed to understand some English. Vietor asked him what the tower frequency was. After a time the man seemed to understand. He ran over to the airport buildings and came back in five minutes with a card on which the frequency was written: 118.1.

Mahmud took the microphone and screamed into it as he had on several occasions: 'I am Captain Martyr Mahmud. . . .' The man in the tower understood nothing, although the Palestinian repeated his speech several times.

Vietor took the microphone. 'I am the German co-pilot,' he said, 'it was not my intention to land here. We are under the command of Captain Martyr Mahmud.'

The man in the tower clearly had no idea what to do. He said he would have to establish contact with his superiors.

Vietor went into the cabin and said to the passengers through the microphone: 'We've landed again. I am not allowed to tell you where, nor do I know what is going to happen. But at least we have solid ground beneath our wheels.' The blinds had to remain drawn. A few young soldiers arrived. They seemed friendly. They placed themselves about 50 feet away from the plane but did not point their guns in its direction. Instead they stood with their backs to it.

Mahmud suddenly laid a hand on Vietor's shoulder and said: 'Your performance has been super-human. I have already said that I would never kill you. Now you can leave the plane.'

Vietor was amazed. For a few seconds he was silent, then replied: 'Thank you, Captain Mahmud, but I'll stay in the plane.'

Mahmud's offer excited him. Somehow he would have to take it further. He went to the cabin microphone and said, first in English and then in German as usual, 'Captain Martyr Mahmud has offered me the chance of leaving the plane, but I'll remain here. I don't want to end up next to the captain in the cupboard.'

Gaby Dillmann and the terrorists laughed. Then Gaby was horrified at her own laughter and thought: 'That's sick. That really is sick humour.'

Vietor was also shocked by what he had said. Not because it was untactful: tact was not an issue any more. But he had made it abundantly clear that he did not trust Mahmud, who might take offence. But Mahmud who remained in the cockpit made no reaction.

As the Landshut landed at 6.22 a.m. local time, in Mogadishu, the Economic Attaché at the German Embassy, Bernd Zeitler, was preparing to end his shift. Since Friday, October 14, when the Somali Embassy in Nairobi had announced that his country was prepared on humanitarian grounds to take the terrorists if they were released from prison, the German Embassy had been on duty for 24 hours a day. Bernd Zeitler immediately passed on the news of the landing to the four other members of the small Embassy and the four military advisers. The German Chargé d'Affair, Dr Michael Libal, 35, was still asleep. His secretary was having a shower. Two other members were shaving.

Libal was the first at the airport – unshaven, in a crumpled shirt he had worn the day before, his tie loose. Together with an assistant, he made contact with the Somali police and set up a direct line to Bonn.

The Somalis did what they could for the Germans. They placed a 16-square-yard office, directly under the tower's control room, at their disposal. As soon as Libal heard that the hijacker was demanding to speak to the representative of the 'Fascist German government' he went to the tower and announced himself over the radio.

Mahmud repeated his 'Martyr Mahmud – Kaffre Gadum' speech. Then he repeated the demands which he had made previously – the release of nine German 'anti-imperialist fighters and two Palestinian companions imprisoned in Turkey.'

It was unclear why he demanded the release of only *nine* terrorist prisoners when the Schleyer kidnappers had mentioned eleven.

The German diplomat could only reply that he had no instructions from his government.

Mahmud said: 'I'm not going to negotiage any more. Our decision is firm. We will blow up the aircraft at 4.00 p.m. with everyone in it if our comrades are not here by then.'

Gaby Dillmann could hear what was being said on the radio. She asked the Palestinian to allow her to come to the microphone. She had to make the situation clear to the German. Clearly he did not believe that Mahmud was serious, she said. Mahmud agreed.

Gaby spoke without any preparation. She quickly reviewed what had happened in the last few days, and begged: 'We have people who are dying of illness, a woman has cancer. One man is a diabetic. The children can't bear it any longer. They and the old people will die soon. We can't survive another day in this heat. We are convinced that Captain Martyr Mahmud will do what he says. Our captain is dead. His body is rotting in the cupboard. We can't bear it any more. How can the German government hesitate? I don't understand it. I don't understand the world any more. Please repeat what I have said, word for word to the Chancellor, for whom I once had such respect.'

Libal could only say that he had understood. He had to make an effort to control his emotions. It was clearly a relief when Mahmud took the microphone again.

After her appeal Gaby Dillmann went from row to row through the cabin. Gently she relayed what information she could and then said out loud to each passenger: 'Now the government knows everything. The Ambassador has understood. I am certain that we will be free in a couple of hours.'

Gaby's optimism rubbed off on the passengers and on the terrorists as well. They became friendly and generous. The hostages were allowed to talk to each other, although they made little use of the privilege. Most of them still avoided doing anything which made them obvious. Each appeared to be nursing his own fear and his own hopes of escaping.

The children were extraordinary. Normally on long hauls children can be a nightmare for stewardesses and fellow travellers, mainly because they are restricted in their movements. Since the hijacking, none of the children had been allowed to move from their seats unless it was to go to the toilet. Yet – except in the first few minutes – none of the ten children had cried or even whined.

They seemed to grasp the danger instinctively. But they did not show any great fear. They behaved better than any of the grown-ups. They watched carefully. The older children comforted their parents from time to time when they felt things were going badly with them. For the little ones, Mahmud had ordered battery-driven toys from Dubai. They played happily in their seats with their noisy robots and whistling locomotives.

The hijackers let them have their way even in threatening situations. The three-year-old Steffen Waida occasionally made Mahmud smile, and the only human gesture which Mahmud allowed himself was to stroke Steffen a few times on the head.

There was one other hostage on board, a very small Yorkshire terrier. He behaved as well as the children. He did not whine or bark. He sat quietly under his owner's seat or on her lap. He only objected once when Gaby Dillmann tried to put him into the stinking toilet because she thought that he too must have a full bladder. Later he went out into the gangway for the first and only time – to pee.

Among the grown-ups, however, there were some difficult passengers. There are always some who when drinks were handed out wanted something extra or different. 'I don't like Cola! Couldn't you bring me a juice, *Fraülein*?' Especially difficult were those who liked alcohol regularly and in large quantities. The boxing promoter, Hans Heyn, could not forget the bottle that the terrorists had taken from him and which was now in the first class section. He would have given anything for it. Its absence seemed harder for him to bear than anything else.

Meanwhile the dispute between Hannelore Piegler and Gaby Dillmann had developed into a private feud. The chief stewardess warned Gaby many times not to overstep her responsibilities. She was against Gaby giving the passengers information. She thought it would be better 'to leave the people to stew.' Gaby ended one of these quiet, intense contretemps with: 'When we're in Frankfurt again, I am going to write a complaint about you!'

Following Gaby's appeal, breakfast arrived at the plane – bread, apples, milk and some tins of yoghourt. Scarcely anyone could eat. The smell from the cupboard was becoming unbearable. On the insistence of the stewardesses, Vietor asked Mahmud to do something. Mahmud allowed him to call the tower to summon an ambulance to take away the body. The stewardesses deployed the rear emergency chute. Mahmud remained in the cockpit. The other three hijackers went to the cupboard. At first they could not manage to shift the body, now stiff with rigor mortis.

The 'small one', Hind Alameh, came to Hartwig Faby, tapped him on the shoulder, and said, very politely as always: 'Could you please help?'

Faby went to the cupboard. He saw the body standing there, shrunken, with its two yellow distorted hands, the blanket still over the head. Faby had never see a dead human being. He gripped the woollen blanket and the shirt and tried to pull it. He tried not to touch anything bloody. He was afraid of the cold skin. The body fell out of the cupboard, its feet jammed in the narrow space. The terrorists pulled the upper part of the body but could not shift it.

Faby said to himself: 'You've got to help.' Suddenly all his feelings switched off. He seized the legs and hauled them out of the cupboard. The blanket slid off the head and Faby saw the bloody face. It made no impression on him. They carried the dead man to the chute and pushed it down. Below, two Somalis took the body to the ambulance.

When Hartwig Faby got back to his seat he broke out into a cold sweat and began to shiver.

Control told Vietor to move to another place, up by the tower. A fire engine showed him the way across the asphalt. It seemed that the sub-structure was a little too soft. He asked the tower: 'Is it firm enough?'

'I think so.'

'You know that? Or do you just think so?'

But he went on following the fire engine.

At about this time a Lufthansa Boeing 707 carrying the Minister of State Hans-Jürgen Wischnewski, the GSG-9 leader, Ulrich Wegener and the psychologist Wolfgang Salewski, was on its way to Mogadishu. They had set off from Dubai, after the Landshut had arrived in Aden. The co-pilot was Rüdeger von Lutzau. The pilot, Rogowski, was at the controls and von Lutzau was at the radio, in contact with Frankfurt and attempting to get landing permission in Aden. It was closed, he was told and in addition 'permission is refused to overfly Aden.'

Lufthansa headquarters in Frankfurt came on the air. 'An important message from the Chancellor to Minister Wischnewski. Minister Wischnewski is authorized to undertake any negotiations with the Yemenis without restrictions.'

A little later the message was filled out a little: 'The authorization to undertake discussions in particular concerns development aid for South Yemen.'

Wischnewski drafted a message to the Yemeni Foreign Minister. He asked for landing permission and offered 'fruitful negotiations'. But the tower gave the standard answer: 'No landing permission.'

The Boeing banked away over the Arabian desert. Jiddah, likewise, did not want anything to do with a 'highly placed German'.

Bonn suggested that they should land in North Yemen: 'There is approval for a flight from there to Aden tomorrow morning for four people. Travelling time will be nine hours.'

Wischnewski thought that such a trip would put him out of the running. Meanwhile landing permission had come through from Jiddah and he ordered the plane down there. In the morning, came the news that the Landshut had landed in Mogadishu. 'I think,' said Wischnewski, 'we could manage something there.'

As they set off at 8.00 a.m. for Somalia, without having received landing permission, Wegener was pessimistic. While he was on the Entebbe raid, the Israelis had told him that the Palestinians had once had a commando base in Somalia. His mood improved when he learned that his team, which had had to return to Germany from Turkey, was already underway and was over the Mediterranean.

Then, to everyone's surprise, Mogadishu gave permission first to overfly Somalia territory and then to land. Schmidt had been speaking to the Somali President, Siad Barre, for an hour.

Rogowski made as short a landing as he could and, with screaming tyres, turned the 707 aside before reaching the hijacked machine to find his space by the airport building.

Wischnewski was taken immediately to see President Barre. Wegener and his aides were taken to the Hotel Curuba. After an hour, Wischnewski arrived at the hotel with the Somali Head of Protocol. He said the head of the Somali police, Abulahi Mahmud Hassan, wanted to speak to Wegener and his Criminal Office colleague, Gerhard Boeden.

They met the police chief in the airport building. The Somali was keyed up. 'They say they're going to blow the plane up at 4.00 p.m. What can we do?'

Wegener replied: 'On no account must the plane be allowed to leave. We have to storm it.' And he sketched out on a piece of paper how he saw the operation.

'You have to practise that immediately with my people,' said the police chief.

Wegener asked: 'Do you have a plane we can practise on?'

There was only a Boeing 707, which lay in a hangar behind the airport building out of sight of the hijackers. Wischnewski encouraged Wegener: 'Come on, old boy, you tell them how to do it. Meantime, we will try to extend the ultimatum.'

Wegener had little hope for the training. The only ladders available were unsafe. They were repaired with strips of wood. Then he found that the Somalis climbed on to the wings too slowly and were too weak to open the doors. Two of them together could not manage it.

'You'll never get anywhere with them,' Boeden commented. Wegener agreed. He went back to the airport building and told Wischnewski so.

'So we'd better talk further,' Wischnewski replied, 'and make sure our men can land here.'

In the 737, the hijackers had noticed the arrival of the Lufthansa. Mahmud asked the tower: 'Who are those people?'

The tower replied: 'A representative of the German government has just landed.'

Mahmud was becoming hoarser and hoarser but he did not shout any more. 'Tell the German representative that there is no question of negotiation,' he said, 'I will only speak to him if he can tell me that the prisoners have been released in Germany.'

The tower asked whether Mahmud wanted lunch brought. Mahmud replied: 'We don't need any more to eat. In three hours, our ultimatum will expire, then everyone in this plane will be either dead or free.'

It had taken all Gaby Dillmann's strength to talk to the German Chargé d'Affair and then reassure the passengers. Now she suddenly felt herself despairing. She asked if she could go and sit in one of the crew's seats in the nose of the aircraft. She did not want to let the passengers see her mood.

When she was alone she took two tranquillizers. She thought that death would be easier to bear. She gulped, near tears, scarcely noticing that Sayeh had sat down beside her.

Sayeh said: 'What's the matter? You've been fantastic so far. You've behaved marvellously.' She offered Gaby a cigarette.

Gaby took it. She was a non-smoker but liked to blow smoke rings sometimes. Now, out of habit, she blew one. The Palestinian wanted to know how she did it. Gaby said: 'Simple, but actually I don't smoke.'

Sayeh laughed and said: 'And I smoke 40 a day, and I can't do it.'

Gaby laughed with her. Suddenly she began to talk about herself, about her grandmother who had a pacemaker and for whom any excitement could be fatal. And about her mother who would be so worried about her safety.

'Believe me,' said Sayeh, 'my mother will be just as worried as yours.'

Gaby wanted to know if she was afraid of dying.

'No,' Sayeh replied. 'We have already died for Palestine.'

Gaby fought back her tears again. 'I want to live, I want to have children. I want to have lots of children. I am afraid that my children will remain unborn. Do you want to have children?'

'Under different circumstances, perhaps,' Sayeh replied, 'but I'm a fighter, I can't think about children. I have to fight so that Palestinian children can come out of their camps and go to their homes.'

Gaby said: 'I've met a man I'm terribly fond of. I want to marry him.'

Sayeh announced that Mahmud and Hind Alameh were engaged. She herself had a friend – one of her comrades – of whom she was very fond.

The two girls discussed men. 'I don't like these hard characters who look good, who think they are terribly strong and keep thumping their own chests,' said Gaby. 'I like men who can cry.'

Sayeh said she could not understand that. She could not stand weaklings. Her man was very strong.

'Thank heavens we don't all have the same taste,' Gaby joked, 'otherwise we'd all be after the same men.' They both laughed. 'My man is incredibly loving and tender but he's not a hero like yours.'

Mahmud called for Sayeh in the cockpit. When she came out, she went straight past Gaby without looking at her. Mahmud took the microphone and said that anyone who wanted to go to the toilet should go immediately. In a quarter of an hour, no one would be allowed to go.

At 3.00, one hour before the ultimatum expired, Mahmud asked the tower whether the German had any news.

The Somali Transport Minister replied: 'We've heard nothing from the German government, but in the name of President Barre, I beg you on humanitarian grounds to free the hostages. The President has promised you free passage.'

Mahmud asked for best wishes and thanks for his hospitality to be passed on to the President, and continued: 'We can't accept his offer. The fascist German government is also lacking in any humanity in its treatment of our imprisoned comrades. What happens now is solely the fault of the fascist German government and of Helmut Schmidt.'

Mahmud told the passengers that their government wanted them to die. Gaby ran to him and asked to be allowed to speak to the German Chargé d'Affair again. The Palestinian gave her the microphone.

In the cockpit of Wischnewski's plane sat Rüdeger von Lutzau, monitoring the radio conversations between the Landshut and the tower. The voices were very distorted. Rüdeger did not know Gaby's voice when he began to write what she was saying:

'We know that this is the end. We know we must die. It will be very hard for us. But we will die as bravely as possible. We're all too young to die, even the oldest of us. We hope that it will be quick, that we suffer no pain. But perhaps it is better to die than live in a world in which human life counts for so little, in a world in which something like this is possible, in which it is more important to keep nine men in prison, than save the lives of 91.

'Tell my family that it was not so bad and tell my friend – his name is Rüdeger von Lutzau – that I love him very much.'

Gaby lost her voice for a moment but then continued: 'I didn't know that the German government contained people like those responsible for our deaths. I hope they can live with their guilt.'

Rüdeger von Lutzau managed to get this last sentence down, then he staggered back, out of the cockpit into the cabin. A Lufthansa doctor on board gave him tranquillizers.

In the Landshut, Gaby told the passengers that the government were not going to act: 'I have no hope any more. Now we can only pray. Pray, pray, pray!'

Harb stood in the gangway and cried: 'Pray to God!' He was holding the women's stockings with which the men had been bound on the flight to Aden.

Mahmud came into the cabin and said he hated to do what he had to do, but the German government left him no choice. He seemed calm and spoke quietly.

The hijackers attached the plastic explosive once again to the walls in front of the first row of seats. Harb ordered the men out singly into the gangway and bound their hands with the stockings. He pulled the knots so tight that the material cut into the skin.

Gaby was still standing in the first class. Sayeh came up to her with a pistol in her hand and screamed: 'Get out! Move!'

'No, I'm not going,' Gaby replied. She remembered that the Palestinian had said that she would shoot the little boy Steffen before the plane went up so that he should not feel anything. Now Gaby was expecting to be shot as well.

Sayeh pushed her down with the gun. Gaby put her hands on the back of the seat as Sayeh began to tie her up. 'I'm sorry,' she said, 'I can't do it very tight.' The knots were so loose that Gaby could have undone them herself.

The other women were tied up. The terrorists were in a hurry. They snatched up the spirit bottles that they had taken from the passengers, knocked the heads off and splashed whisky and Spanish brandy on the carpet, and then on the passengers themselves. Then they opened the perfume bottles as well and sprinkled the contents about.

Gaby tried to pray: 'Dear God, if you are there do not leave us.' She tried to remember the Lord's Prayer and finally managed to say it right through. She thought of Rüdeger and of the children they might have had. She began to repeat 'Our Father' as quickly as she could. She remembered the last time she had prayed. She had been eight years old. It was when she lost her house key and was afraid that her Granny would hit her.

When Harb saw that she was praying, he smiled for a moment, and then called out: 'All of you pray to your God!' Almost everyone began to do so.

Faby was still trying to observe and analyse the situation. Gaby had told him that Sayeh was going to shoot his friend's son before the explosion. He watched Steffen continuously. He thought of his wife. He tried to work out how much his life insurance was worth. He realized that he had not made a will. Perhaps he ought to write one, but then he realized that it would be burnt. He thought that nothing much had happened in his life and that he had never bothered enough about his friends, that God could not let him leave this life yet. He did not want to pray because he was not religious, but he nevertheless caught himself trying to bargain for his life. He promised God to give up smoking and never have any more extra-marital affairs.

Vietor found he could not concentrate on praying. He counted the minutes. Mahmud had broken his watch in Dubai, but just across from him, somebody had put their watch in the rack on the back of the seat. He watched the second hand.

Lilo Cramer was repeating one of her prayers: 'My ancestors, Rachel, Leah and Sarah, take me to you and receive me blessed into heaven.'

Ten minutes before the ultimatum was due to expire, Mahmud went into the cockpit again and spoke to the tower. He said in a quiet, almost solemn voice: 'We, the Halimeh Commando, are fighting fascist governments throughout the world together with the Somali people. We are fighting shoulder to shoulder with the Somali people against the fascist Ethiopians. We do not want to spill Somali blood on Somali soil. Please remove all your soldiers and vehicles because we are going to blow the plane up.'

'Yes, we'll pull the soldiers back,' the tower replied. 'Thank you for thinking of it. But we need a little time.'

Three minutes before the ultimatum expired, Mahmud asked: 'Are the Somali soldiers away yet?'

The tower replied: 'No, not yet. The Transport Minister wants to speak to you.'

'Please, Mister Minister, speak,' said Mahmud.

'It's not possible to pull back the soldiers so quickly,' said the Transport Minister. 'Communications are bad, can you give us a little more time?'

'The ultimatum expires in a few seconds,' said Mahmud, 'I can't decide that alone. We are a Commando. We have to discuss it.' A little while later he radioed: 'We have decided three to one that the ultimatum should be extended by half an hour. We don't want to kill any Somalis. Please thank President Barre again.'

In the airport building, Frau Gisela Libal brought her husband some clean underwear and a freshly ironed shirt. Wischnewski, who despite the tropical heat was dressed in a dark suit with a neatly knotted tie, radiated calm. He did not believe that the hijackers would fulfil their threats. He saw his views confirmed by the extension of the ultimatum. Then the Somali police chief, Abulahi Mahmud Hassan, came up agitated. He asked: 'Who will take the responsibility if the machine goes up? I can't.'

Wischnewski too became unsettled. He whispered to his people: 'As long as they don't try anything.' He feared that the Somalis might attempt to storm the machine. He told the tower to tell the hijackers he would have something to say to them in a little while.

Meanwhile, Wischnewski had worked out a plan of campaign with Salewski to make the terrorists hold their hands. Libal and Salewski went to the tower. Libal called up the Landshut and said he had important information.

Mahmud said: 'What's it about? I've already said that I cannot negotiate! I'm only interested in the freedom of my comrades!'

Libal said: 'We have agreed to your demands. The prisoners can now be released and are to be taken to Frankfurt airport.'

'At last, at last,' said Mahmud, 'you've understood at last, but it's almost too late.'

'We're prepared to give in to your demands,' said Libal, 'but it's a long way from here to Germany. We need time.'

'Tell me the distance from Germany to Mogadishu.'

'One moment please,' said Libal, 'I'll find out.'

'Yes, find out, but hurry.'

In the pause that followed he added: 'What about the withdrawal of the soldiers? Where is the German?'

A Somali in the tower reassured him: 'One moment, one moment. Yes, he's coming back now.' Libal said that the distance was 7,000 kilometres. Mahmud said he would call up again shortly.

Sayeh came into the cabin, she went up to Gaby and released her bonds. Gaby shouted: 'We're free! We're free!'

Hind Alameh picked up Steffen Waida and hugged him. The terrorists released the stewardesses and Vietor. The passengers began to cry, some from joy and many from pain, for the bonds had cut their circulation and their hands were swollen. The hostages called to be released as soon as possible.

Mahmud laughed and said: 'At last your government has

understood. Now the lady with a hair appointment can keep it.' He called Vietor into the cockpit and once again became serious. He asked the co-pilot how far it was from Germany to Mogadishu.

Vietor took out a handbook, opened it at the map section and measured with a biro: '50° north – 60 miles per degree – about 3,000 miles.'

Mahmud asked how long it would take to fly that distance. Vietor replied: 'For a 707 flying at 400 knots – 8 hours, depending on the wind.'

The Palestinian called Libal on the radio and asked: 'When will the prisoners be here? We don't want to wait until tomorrow.'

'Tomorrow morning would be a good time.'

'No,' replied Mahmud, 'that's too long for me. It's seven hours flying time. I'll give you another three on top of that. That makes 2.00 a.m.'

Libal said: 'That's a reasonable suggestion. We can manage that.'

Mahmud was clearly taken aback by the German's readiness to agree so quickly. He insisted: 'We're not giving up anything else. We're still prepared to blow up the plane. If you think this is going to be a second Entebbe, you're wrong.'

In the airport building the German group knew that the GSG-9 unit was already circling Djibouti and would shortly receive landing permission from the Somalis.

After their return from Turkey the GSG-9 commandos had taken up their normal duties in Hangelaar. They were to do shooting and sport that day. Nobody believed that they were going to see any further action.

On Sunday, there was a new order from Bonn. Two units were to make ready to fly to the south-east. The plane took off on Monday without a fixed destination. It was refuelled in Crete. The men mentally prepared themselves for a long tour of duty rather than for an assault. They were told to fly to Djibouti, where they circled waiting for landing permission from Mogadishu. As their fuel ran out and the hope died in Bonn that the Somalis would allow German troops on to their soil, the plane descended towards Djibouti to refuel.

During the descent, the order came to continue to Mogadishu. The pilot hauled the plane back up again and estimated fuel reserves and flying time. They realized that they could do it if they flew over the Ethiopian war zone which was technically a closed area.

At 8.00 p.m. local time the 707 landed at Mogadishu, down to its last few hundred litres of fuel and, contrary to all regulations, with the wind behind it. All the lights were out. The plane rolled rapidly over to the military section of the airport. It was not noticed by the hijackers.

Ulrich Wegener greeted his deputy, Klaus Blätte, who had arrived with the rest of the unit from Hangelaar: 'Now it's for real. Get everything unpacked. I'm going to see how the land lies.'

It took two hours to unload GSG-9's equipment and it took Wegener two hours to complete his reconnaissance. Creeping up behind a low sand dune, he got to within 30 yards of the Landshut, then he returned to Wischnewski.

'We're going to do it,' he told him confidently, 'but don't ask for any details.'

Wischnewski nodded: 'Okay, I'll leave that to the experts. Just tell me what's happening a little bit before the attack.'

Wegener told the Somali police chief something of his plan: it had been agreed that the action – codenamed Magic Fire – should be presented as a joint Somali-German operation.

In the Landshut, Mahmud himself had helped to untie the last of the passengers. He asked if anyone was in pain. Many of the hostages said they were. The Palestinian said he was sorry. 'but your government . . . they would have killed us. We would have died together like a family.' He massaged a few of the passengers' hands, raised their arms and showed them how to stimulate the circulation.

The passengers seemed to have lost their fear and hate of the hijackers. Mahmud received only agreement when he made the West German government responsible for the sorrows of the last five days. Gaby Dillmann summed up their mood when she gave an improvised speech, laughing and angry at the same time: 'What do those people in Bonn

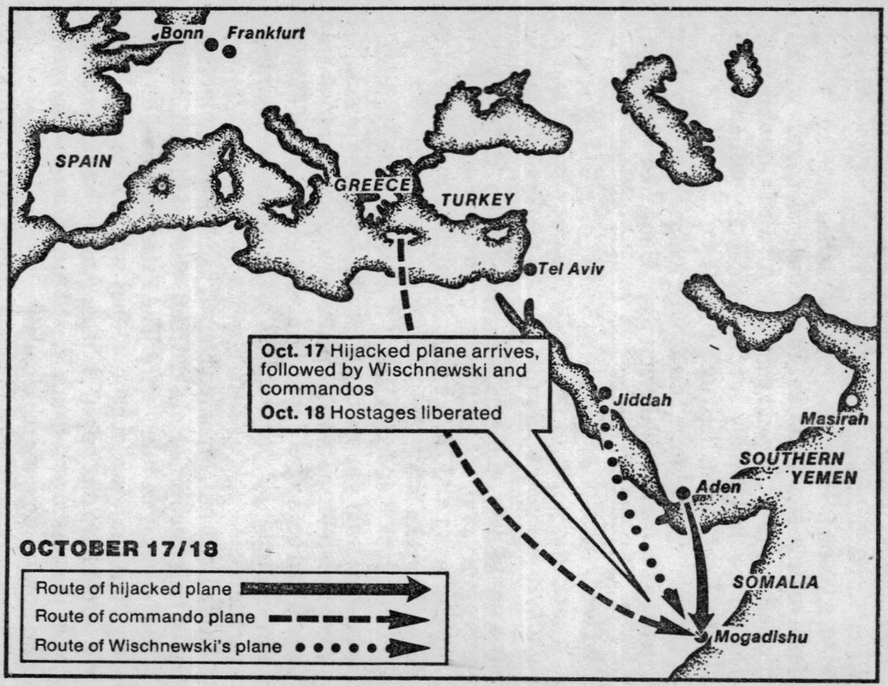
Bonn
Frankfurt
SPAIN
GREECE
TURKEY
Tel Aviv
Jiddah
Masirah
SOUTHERN YEMEN
Aden
SOMALIA
Mogadishu
Oct. 17 Hijacked plane arrives, followed by Wischnewski and commandos
Oct. 18 Hostages liberated
OCTOBER 17/18
Route of hijacked plane
Route of commando plane
Route of Wischnewski's plane

think they're doing sitting on their fat back-sides and playing with our lives? I have to admit something terrible – I'm an S.P.D. member. Once I really revered Schmidt. But I'll resign as soon as I get home. I'll make a scandal of the whole thing. We'll mobilize the press.' Passengers and terrorists applauded together.

Even Jürgen Vietor found that he no longer hated Mahmud, despite the threats to shoot him and the murder of his colleague. 'He's not a killer. He doesn't want to kill,' Vietor thought. 'He's lucky that he doesn't have to kill us now.'

Wischnewski's group meanwhile did their best to apply Salewski's advice to keep the terrorists busy and always give them solid new hope. Salewski and the German ambassador took turns at the microphone. First, they said they were going to fetch the Turkish ambassador to arrange that the Palestinians imprisoned in Turkey should also be released. Later, they admitted their 'discovery' that there was no Turkish ambassador in Somalia. They tried to confuse Mahmud with different time zones, making him do calculations several times over.

They had before them an accurate flight plan of the Frankfurt-Mogadishu haul, complete with radio beacons and times. They could keep the hijacker continuously informed as to where the fictitious plane with the prisoners was or should be. They always tried to give their words a slight gloss of uncertainty, which Mahmud ignored.

Mahmud and the 'small one'. Hind Alameh, made two places available for Vietor in the first-class section and said he should sleep. When Vietor lay down, they brought him a blanket and some cushions.

The two went back to the cockpit. Vietor was not able to sleep and watched through the open door as Mahmud stroked and whispered to Hind Alameh until the girl went to sleep with her head on his chest.

In Bonn, Schmidt was playing chess. He and the other members of the crisis staff were racked with tension. The link with Mogadishu had been broken. It went via Rome and there was either a holiday or a pro-Palestinian operator had broken the link.

In Wischnewski's operation room, the silent radio had a calming effect. One of Wischnewski's advisors said: 'Let's hope they don't get through in a hurry or we'll have Maihofer asking the wind direction every ten minutes.'

Towards midnight, scouts, under Klaus Blätte's leadership, approached the Landshut. Behind a sand dune 30 yards away they watched the plane through infra-red glasses and relayed their findings through a walkie-talkie to Wegener. They confirmed that there were probably two hijackers in the cockpit. There were: Mahmud and Hind Alameh.

At about 1.15 a.m. specialists with grenade-throwers were in position as were marksmen. The two Englishmen of the S.A.S., Major Alistair Morrison and Sergeant Barry Davies, who had accompanied Wegener from Dubai, were preparing their own 'fireworks'.

The next difficult phase of Operation Magic Fire began: the stealthy approach to the plane by the storm troopers.

Wegener gave last minute instructions. On the command 'Heads down!' he said, anyone left standing in the plane was to be shot. He assumed, or rather hoped, that the instinctive reaction of the hostages would be to throw themselves down or duck, although he knew that this hope had not been completely realized at Entebbe, where a hostage had stood and been hit. In addition, he assumed that the Arabs would put up little resistance to a successful surprise attack.

Wearing dark blue and green pants and shirts, their faces blackened with camouflage paint, the commandos crept stealthily to the rear of the hijacked plane. Some of the men were armed with pistols; others clutched MP5 sub-machine guns. One group crouched in readiness beneath the tail while others took up positions under the wings and nose. Then metal ladders were quietly propped against the fuselage and magnetic explosive charges were placed around the front and rear doors on the right side of the aircraft.

In the Landshut, Gaby Dillmann borrowed Mahmud's comb and began to untangle a little girl's hair. She gave her some plaits and showed her the results in a small hand mirror. It was a trick mirror: if you looked at it in the right way a great grinning face stared out. She gave it to the 'fat one', Suhaila Sayeh, who showed it to her companions. Everyone laughed.

Mahmud ordered the passengers, threateningly, not to give any information about him and the other commandos. He handed out Lufthansa envelopes on which every hostage had to write down his or her name and address. He collected the envelopes again and pushed them into a bag.

Then he gave another short speech: 'We're freedom fighters and not terrorists or robbers. We don't want your money or your valuables.' He said that anyone could come forward and check whether anything valuable had been taken from the hand luggage. Fifteen passengers did actually go into the first class compartment to look through their purses and count their money.

One old lady who found her money untouched, turned to Gaby Dillmann and said: 'My valuables are still safe in my handbag but I brought a basket of vegetables from Majorca. I haven't seen it. It's not important, but I would like to know where it is.'

Suddenly Mahmud learned there was a fire burning a little way from the plane. He ordered the checking to cease.

Rüdeger von Lutzau was sitting in his co-pilot's seat in his Boeing 707. He was recording the radio exchanges. From his place on the right-hand side of the plane, he could see clearly into the Landshut. When the fire started, he realized it was a diversion started by the Somalis. They wanted to entice as many terrorists as possible into the cockpit. He knew that in a few minutes, Gaby would be either free or dead. His Lufthansa colleagues crowded into the cockpit with him.

In the cockpit of the Landshut, Mahmud scarcely had any time to consider the fire. The tower told him that the plane with the prisoners had just taken off from Cairo, where it had made a stop over. He was asked the conditions of the exchange. Mahmud read from a card: 'The incoming plane should be positioned so that we can supervise everything. It will be surrounded by Somali soldiers. The transport minister will supervise the exchange. Our released comrades must emerge singly. For every comrade, we will release a group of passengers. . . .'

It was 2.07 a.m., 23 minutes before Mahmud's final

deadline expired. At that moment the emergency doors over the wings were blown open, and the commandos tossed in the English 'stun' grenades. The GSG-9 men kept their eyes closed for several seconds. The cabin was filled by blinding light and a noise that left those inside deafened. Then Wegener opened the forward door at the head of one group. Two other groups attacked over the wings. Almost instantaneously, men with blackened faces were in at the rear of the plane.

The passengers were overwhelmed by the detonations. They heard German voices: 'Heads down! Where are the swine?' And then shots. No one understood what was happening. Many thought it was all over. They ducked down in their seats, trying to get on to the floor as bullets cracked back and forth over the seats.

Hind Alameh died instantly. Mahmud, fatally wounded by two 9-mm bullets, managed to throw two hand grenades before he died. They were home-made ones and blew up without injuring anyone seriously. The 'fat one', Suhaila Sayeh, ran into the toilet and shot once through the closed door. Her fire was returned instantly. Inside, she fell, wounded.

Wabil Harb shot with his pistol until he too slumped to the floor, wounded and unconscious.

Vietor thought, at the first explosion, 'This really is it.' He flattened himself on the floor and tried to push his head under a seat. His next inconsequential thought was: 'I've lost my hair.' He saw his toupee, which he had had on for the last five days, in front of him on the floor.

Gaby Dillmann could not get on the floor because beside her sat a fat lady. Her legs were in the gangway. When the first hand-grenade exploded near her, she felt a blow and something hot. She thought: 'My leg's gone. It doesn't matter.' At first there was no pain. But when she tried to move her toes, it hurt. Then she knew at least that her leg was still there.

Somebody shouted: 'Come on! get out! Quick! Quick!' Gaby Dillmann ran doubled up to the emergency exit, tumbled out on to a wing and was led over to a ladder. On the last few rungs her legs gave out. Someone helped her up. It was Wegener. Gaby was crying. Wegener said as he carried her to an ambulance: 'Now everything's okay, my girl. Nothing else can happen now.' Gaby sobbed, 'Everything's still there. . . . My leg and all my toes. . . . It just burns a bit.'

Rüdeger von Lutzau heard the attack begin. He leant forward to see if he could see anything, but had to rely on a colleague who was sitting on his right. 'Now the first passengers are coming out by the rear steps. . . . Now I can see a movement in the emergency exits. . . . They're coming out over the wings and running away.' Any moment, thought Rüdeger, the Landshut will explode. He still imagined it disappearing in a ball of fire.

Then his captain came running over to the plane and cried: 'Come on! Gaby's alive! She's only slightly wounded.' Rüdeger von Lutzau ran across the airfield. He saw her sitting on a blanket. He knelt down beside her and, at last, broke down. Gaby put her arms around him and said: 'It's really nothing terribly bad. I'm all there still.'

Rüdeger stopped weeping for a moment and whispered: 'We'll get married before Christmas.'

'Yes,' Gaby replied, 'but in a church. That much I've promised God. We have to return to the Church.'

Later it struck her that Rüdeger had proposed to her just as she had imagined he ought to, on his knees. Only the flowers and the suit were missing.

Operation Magic Fire had begun at 2.07 a.m. At 2.12 a.m. troops radioed control: 'Springtime! Springtime!' The code word for the end of the operation. A little later a radio message was sent to Bonn. 'Four opponents down; hostages freed, four slightly wounded hostages; one trooper slightly wounded.'

Wabil Harb was carried out of the aircraft. He was still breathing. At the top of the steps, he tumbled off his stretcher and fell almost six feet on to the concrete. He was placed back on the stretcher but died a few minutes later.

From her stretcher, Suhaila Sayeh stretched out two fingers in the victory sign. She shouted out in English: 'Kill me! Please kill me!' And then in Arabic: 'Long live free Palestine!'

The 10-year-old Stefan Röhll saw Harb's body, he

shouted: 'Look Mummy, that's the nice one. He's dead.'

'You can hardly recognize him,' Birgitt Röhll replied.

'Oh, yes you can,' Stefan replied emphatically, 'I recognize him by his nice boots.'

Hasse Heyn wandered across the airfield and into the airport building. At last he found what he was looking for: a German with a bottle of whisky beside him. He asked for a strong drink. The German was surprised. He gave him some whisky in a paper cup and said: 'But couldn't you put some Cola or something like that with it?'

Vietor was talking to a Somali officer in the main hall: 'I am the pilot,' he said, 'I have to go back to the plane urgently.' The officer got hold of a car for him.

The car halted 50 yards from the plane. Vietor said: 'I'll be back in five minutes.' He climbed into the Landshut. There was no one else near. Even in the entrance he noticed how terribly the cabin stank. The lights were on. The auxiliary generator was still running. Vietor thought: 'I'd better switch off,' and then: 'Well, it's not up to me any more.'

He went along the rows, knelt down and looked on the floor. He found his toupee immediately. He put it on and went back to the car.

The freed hostages and victorious commandos arrived back in Cologne in the early afternoon. They were given an ecstatic reception. Brass bands played. Radio stations put on the *Ode to Joy* from Beethoven's Ninth Symphony. One television commentator summed up the national euphoria: 'It feels good to be a German today.'

5. SUICIDE AT STAMMHEIM

On the evening of October 17, in Stammheim Prison, eight men and a woman were on duty supervising the 800 prisoners. At 11.00 p.m., Orderly Wilhelm Kölz made his way to Section III, where the cells of the Baader-Meinhof prisoners lay, on the seventh floor, to hand out some pills. It was a complicated procedure. The night watchman on the seventh floor telephoned down to the central guard room, where the television monitoring system was, to switch off Section III's alarm system. Kölz, with his medical trolley and accompanied by four executive officers, went through four doors which all had to be unlocked individually. Their progress was checked on closed-circuit television. They halted at Jan-Carl Raspe's cell, 716. One official went into a bullet-proof glass cabin and put her hand on an alarm telephone, ready for trouble. A mattress placed against the cell door to deaden sound was removed. The cell's two locks were opened and the three remaining officials stood back, behind the orderly. Kölz gave Raspe two tranquillizers. Raspe thanked him. The men retreated, the cell was locked again and the mattress replaced.

Then it was Baader's turn in cell 719. Baader was sitting on the floor and chewing a piece of bread. He stood up and swallowed the tablets. It was the first time in weeks that he had not sworn at the officials.

Gudrun Ensslin, in cell 720, had not asked for anything and no one opened the flap of her door to look in. Recently, she had taken to throwing cold water into the faces of anyone who checked on her.

Irmgard Möller, in 725, was not due for anything, either. Kölz and the other officials left the block. The alarm system was switched on again and the four Baader-Meinhof prisoners were alone once more.

But there was no peace – indeed there could not be – in the echoing concrete building. The radio system, which each prisoner could hear through ear-phones, was soon switched off, as always at 11.30 p.m. But many prisoners kept their portable radios on and held them against the cell windows so that other prisoners could hear. It was the night of the Mogadishu raid. The four-square walls echoed the news; everyone could hear what was going on, even the Baader-Meinhof prisoners up on the seventh floor.

The guards knew about this, of course, but it did not worry them much. Stammheim was the 'securest prison in the world' according to Baden-Württemberg Justice Minister, Traugott Bender. Besides, after Schleyer's abduction on September 5, police from the Baden-Württemberg Criminal Office had begun to check over the Baader-Meinhof cells for themselves. On September 23, they found a Minox camera hidden in a jar of Baader's coffee. On the orders of the *Land* Justice Ministry, their radios and televisions were taken away. They were forbidden to receive letters or newspapers. They were not allowed visitors. All of them, except Gudrun Ensslin, were moved regularly to other cells. They were separated by empty cells and could not contact each other by knocking. After the law banning any contact – between the terrorists themselves and with the outside world – came into effect on October 1, the Baader-Meinhof prisoners were unable even to see their lawyers. In addition, Baader, Raspe, Ensslin and Möller were forbidden to receive laundry, borrow books from the prison library or buy any extra food.

On Tuesday, October 18, at 7.41 a.m., two officers, Gerhard Stoll and Willi Stapf, arrived at cell 716 with the breakfast trolley, which incorporated special baffles to prevent any attempt at poisoning. Breakfast was to have been coffee, bread and a boiled egg.

As they opened the door, the two men saw Raspe on his bed, gasping, leaning back against the wall.

The prison officers slammed the door, and gave the alarm to the medical unit. Orderly Edgar Jost summoned an ambulance and somebody called the senior duty inspector, Erich Götz, who burst into the cell with his senior orderly, Christop Listner, and a few other assistants. In his right hand Raspe, who was unconscious, held a pistol. Götz snatched up the weapon from Raspe's half-opened fingers, and lay it in a chequered dishcloth that one of his assistants held out to him. Raspe had a single bullet wound in the head.

Orderly Adolf Soukop felt Raspe's pulse – it was still just detectable – and ran down to Baader's cell. He was lying half in shadow about a yard from the door, on his back. Soukop felt his pulse and found he was dead with bullet wounds in the head.

'Let's get over to Ensslin,' he said to other officers near him. Cell 720 lay in darkness. Soukop called in, frightened that Ensslin, too, might have a pistol and might be ready to use it. There was no answer. Then, behind a curtain at the window, he saw Ensslin's feet dangling a few inches off the floor.

At that moment the Deputy Medical Officer, Dr. Wladislaw Majerowicz, came into the cell. Soukop ran on and opened cell 725, Irmgard Möller's. She was lying doubled up on the mattress with her face to the wall, a blanket pulled up to her chin.

'I pulled back the blanket,' Soukop said afterwards, 'and found my hands soaked in blood . . . I pulled up her T-shirt and saw that there were stab wounds in the region of her heart.' But the wounds were superficial. Pulse and blood-pressure were normal. Dr. Majerowicz, a Pole by origin, who had been in Stammheim since 1973, said: 'She was not in danger. I gave her an injection to help her circulation, but there had been little loss of blood. She was quite conscious, although she was in some pain.'

At 8.09 a.m. the hospital ambulance carrying Raspe, accompanied by three police cars, streaked away from Stammheim, arriving 11 minutes later at the Neurosurgical Department of Stuttgart's Katharine Hospital. Raspe was X-rayed and then wheeled into the operating theatre.

At 8.27 a.m. the hospital emergency phone rang again. Stammheim wanted another ambulance, this time for Irmgard Möller. She was taken to Stuttgart's Robert Bosch Hospital. Later, she was flown by police helicopter to the Surgical Department of Tübingen University Clinic. It turned out she had stabbed herself with a serrated, but blunt prison knife, and damaged the pericardium, the membranous sac that surrounds the heart. She recovered after a minor operation.

At 9.40 a.m. Raspe was declared dead.

Schmidt heard the news from Stammheim just before a special cabinet meeting at 9.06. 'I felt as though I had been hit by a club,' he said. 'I was shocked, appalled. After the raid there had been an immense feeling of relief – and six hours later, *this*.'

The political consequences were potentially disastrous, as everyone immediately saw. West Germany could suffer for years from the Stammheim scandal, and from the mythology that could spring up about the deaths. A few hours later, the first German property abroad was in flames. Within a few days – according to a rapid poll – millions in other west European countries believed that the terrorists had been murdered.

To counteract the effects of the deaths – to quash the rumours that Baader and Raspe had been murdered and then positioned to suggest suicide – Justice Minister Hans-Jochen Vogel immediately suggested that international observers be invited to the post-mortem. The *Land* Justice Ministry in Stuttgart agreed. Invitations went out to Professor Wilhelm Holczabeck in Vienna, Professor Hans-Peter Hartmann in Zürich and Professor André at the University of Liège.

The first police official at Stammheim was Detective Superintendent Gosbert Müller. He arrived at 8.30 a.m. and ordered that no one was to be allowed into the cells until the international observers had arrived.

So Gudrun Ensslin remained where she was, hanging by the flex of her record player from the window bars. Baader was left on his back. From his initial examination, Dr.

Majerowicz concluded that both had died between 6.00 a.m. and 7.00 a.m.

At 1.20 p.m. Professor Hartmann arrived from Zürich by helicopter; at 2.30 p.m. Professor Holczabek came in from Vienna; and by 6.00 p.m. André had arrived. The initial examination of the corpses by Professor Joachim Rauschke from Stuttgart and Professor Hans-Joachim Mallach, from Tübingen, began at 4.00 p.m.

On Baader's right hand there were blood stains and powder marks – text book evidence that he had shot himself.

The doctors also found every indication that Ensslin, still hanging at the window, had died by hanging. The look of the skin was indicative, as Professor Rauschke later explained: 'When a body is hanging, gravity forces the blood downwards; it settles in the lower parts of the body and creates discolourations, particularly in the arms, legs and chin. The discolourations in this case were consistent with hanging.'

Watched by the three foreign professors and the four Baader-Meinhof lawyers, surrounded by other lawyers and policemen, the two German professors began the post-mortem at 10.00 p.m., in the morgue of the Bergfriedhof, Tübingen.

Raspe's wounds had already been examined by the two doctors shortly after his death in the Katharine Hospital. The test for powder marks on Raspe's right hand was positive.

It was harder to assess Baader's wound. The bullet had entered at the hair-line at the back of the head and re-emerged at the hair-line in the front. Baader must therefore have killed himself by shooting himself in the back of the head. This method of suicide is not impossible, but it is extremely rare. In Austria, for instance, it has been known only twice in the last ten years. The previous comparable case in Germany, according to the literature, was in 1931. The professors felt themselves forced to consider, therefore, whether suicide was the only possible conclusion to which they could come.

For Baader to have been killed by somebody else, the murderer would have needed to hold Baader's right hand, which in its turn held the weapon, and turned it towards the back of his head. This would have been the only way for the blood and powder marks to have been made consistent with those of suicide. In addition Baader would need to have been unconscious, but in that case there would have been signs of blows, strangulation, or binding. If he had been made unconscious by gas, tablets or injections, the biochemical effects on his internal organs would have been unequivocal. There were no signs of violence and none of chemical interference.

Rauschke and Mallach concluded that suicide was the only possible cause of death.

Likewise Ensslin's body was examined for pressure marks which would have resulted if she had been hung up by others. There were no such signs. The scientists concluded unequivocally that Ensslin had been still living when the flex was placed round her neck, that there were no signs of violence and therefore that no one else was involved.

There were, however, some scratches in the region of her left breast, marks on the edge of the left thumb and on both knees and a blood stain on the middle finger of her left hand. How did they arise? Rauschke explained: 'Strangulation occurs in a number of stages. After about eight seconds, unconsciousness ensues; in the second stage, which can last up to a minute, convulsions occur which are very similar to those of an epileptic fit and can be extremely violent. The effusions and skin wounds arose during these convulsions.'

The two doctors continued the post-mortem until 4.00 a.m. without any objections from the Baader-Meinhof lawyers. Isolated and hostile, the four stood in the background of the morgue, watched at every step. When Hans-Heinz Heldmann, Baader's lawyer, walked into a next-door room where refreshments were available and asked for a Coco Cola he was ordered out again by one of the public prosecutors. In the view of the police, the detectives and the prosecutors, it was only the lawyers who could have smuggled the weapons into the prison.

The four went on to Bonn and gave a press conference at the Tulpenfeld Hotel in which they strongly and skilfully suggested to the international press, without mentioning the word murder, that there was no question of suicide.

They were not unsuccessful. Many foreign journalists found the story of the two pistols completely incredible – and not without reason. It was a story that became more incredible as time went on.

Soon after the deaths, a saucer-sized transistor radio was found in Raspe's cell, wrapped in a pullover behind his bed. That evening the *Land* Justice Minister, Traugott Bender, sacked the prison head, Hans Nusser, and his deputy, Ulrich Schreitmüller. Bender accused Schreitmüller of sanctioning disastrous lapses in Stammheim's security. Schreitmüller claimed that nobody had been made responsible for security in the prison.

Gradually the true dimensions of the security problem on the seventh floor emerged as experts from the *Land* Criminal Office, the Federal Criminal Office and Stuttgart's Post Office Divisional Administration pulled up floors, tore down walls, and removed wash basins. Their discoveries of communication systems and a variety of hiding places for weapons forced the resignation of Bender.

A parliamentary committee of inquiry, set up on October 20, established details that revealed a staggering combination of ingenuity on the part of the prisoners and lack of imagination and/or rigorousness on the part of the authorities. Raspe was the key figure. In prison he had not only learnt Russian, but also studied computers and electronics. He had subscribed to a dozen technical journals to extend his education – clearly with some success. All four cells were linked by a first-class communication system, which remained unaffected by the ban on personal contact and remained undiscovered despite the supposedly daily supervision by the prison officials.

Raspe's cell, 716, was painted yellow (like the others) and had a grey P.V.C. floor. Behind the bed, police found a hole in the corner of the outer wall into which Raspe's pistol had fitted exactly. The hole had been covered over with wood and plaster so neatly and so firmly that it did not sound hollow when knocked.

There was a similar hiding place in cell 715 to which Baader was moved on October 4. He must have found a way of taking his gun with him when he was moved back to his old cell, 719. There he hid his gun in a record player, which went on working (as the provincial Criminal Office found when they checked the machine after Schleyer's kidnapping).

More remarkable still, when an electricity expert from the Post Office in Stuttgart examined the loud speaker he found that it had been turned into a microphone, wired to transmit into the electrical system.

Three of the prisoners (not Raspe) simply plugged in their headphones to create their own one-way communications network.

Raspe's cell was divided from the others by a staircase and was on a different circuit. He could not therefore take part in the radio link between Baader, Ensslin and Möller. Raspe communicated with Baader through an electric-razor circuit which could be used for shaving only twice a day, for an hour each time; for the rest of the time it made an effective communications network.

In Irmgard Möller's cell – as in all cells – there was a socket into which the prisoner could plug earphones to listen to the prison radio. But Möller's turned out to be a special socket: through it ran the leads to the radio outlets in Ensslin's and Baader's cells.

After the Schleyer kidnapping, the plug was disconnected by the prison electrician. Hardly was he out of the door when Irmgard Möller reconnected it. From then on she was able to listen to the prison radio, as were Ensslin and Baader from 5.30 a.m. to 11.30 in the evening. For the rest of the night, Raspe could relay any information he gathered on his transistor radio.

Nor was that all. When cell 723 (until mid-August occupied by Helmut Pohl) was examined, experts found behind the panel of the socket a packet, one inch wide and five inches long. It contained nine ounces of explosive, enough, if used correctly, to blow a hole in the wall, or to build two powerful hand grenades.

Detonators were found when the wall in Ingrid Schubert's cell was broken down. They were neatly packed together with some matches and several more ounces of explosive.

Thereupon the new Justice Minister, Guntram Palm, ordered all non-weight-bearing walls in Section III to be torn down.

A number of times the prisoners summoned officials of the Criminal Office – there were six visits between September 13 and October 15. The police were always hopeful that there would be some clue to the Schleyer kidnappers. But the Baader-Meinhof members were only prepared to talk about their exchange, though they also began to suggest the idea of their own deaths.

For instance, on October 9, Baader told a police official: 'If the delaying tactics don't end soon, the prisoners will decide things for themselves. The security organizations will then be faced with the development in which they, the cheaters, will be cheated. The prisoners don't intend to accept the prison situation any longer. They will in the future not be available to the government.'

On October 17, Gudrun Ensslin asked to see the prison chaplains. She told the two men that in her cell there lay a red folder with three letters which on no account should be allowed to fall into the hands of the Federal Prosecutor. She told the priests that the letters should be mentioned to her lawyer, Otto Schily, or to her parents because, she said, she and the others were to be executed. 'You don't know how things work here,' she told them, 'those who are here don't do that sort of thing; others come from outside.' There were no letters, and the two clerics later concluded that her words were intended to give the impression of a 'murder conspiracy' in the case of suicide.

Baader followed right through on this ploy. Before he killed himself, he put two shots into the cell wall and reloaded the eight-shot magazine. Moreover, Baader, who was left-handed, then used his *right* hand to turn the gun on to the back of his head and pull the trigger. A suicide who bothered to reload, and then shoot himself in the back of the neck with his wrong hand? No wonder the whole thing was regarded as incredible. That was the way it was planned.

That the Baader-Meinhof prisoners committed suicide is not, therefore, in any doubt. For those closely involved there never was any doubt. But disturbing questions remain unanswered. How did the prisoners obtain guns, ammunition, and explosive? How did these escape detection? It is almost beyond the bounds of possibility that the prisoners brought such items into prison with them; it must be considered almost certain therefore that outsiders were involved. The field of possible accomplices is not extensive. Those under suspicion must include the prison staff, the *Land* authorities responsible for security, and, in particular, the Baader-Meinhof lawyers. To establish the accomplices will be a vital step in ensuring West Germany's security against future acts of terrorism.

Hanns Martin Schleyer's death dragged out for three long days for his family. On Sunday, October 16, at 9.00 a.m. the final ultimatum set by the kidnappers for the freeing of the R.A.F. prisoners expired. In the past few weeks many ultimatums had expired without the kidnappers carrying out their threat to murder their hostage. But this, the seventh ultimatum, had a different quality. With the hijacking of the Landshut and the government's obvious decision to storm the plane, those close to Hanns Martin Schleyer had begun a final countdown.

The optimism with which his family had followed the Landshut's progress vanished. At first they could not believe that the government would risk the lives of 87 other hostages. Jörg, the youngest son, told friends on the day of the hijacking: 'Now we can hope again.'

On Sunday, when the radio announced the murder of Schumann in Aden, this hope evaporated. That Sunday the family celebrated Arndt Schleyer's 29th birthday. It was a belated celebration: his birthday had actually been on September 14. Over wine, the family decided on yet one more attempt to save their father, by contacting the kidnappers direct. Hanns-Eberhard called Denis Payot and asked him to pass a message on to the hijackers. He gave no details of his suggestion, which involved another attempt to buy his father's freedom with several million marks provided by Daimler-Benz and colleagues in industry. There was no response.

On Monday night, as the assault loomed closer, Jörg left home to find out more about the events in Mogadishu. Towards midnight, he was at the South German Radio where he heard the news of the successful assault. He showed immediate delight, then suddenly fell silent and said, 'I've just realized that means a death sentence for my father.' He returned home in the early hours. At 8.30 a.m., his mother knocked on his door to tell him about the Stammheim suicides. Neither of them had any hope left and each offered the other what comfort they could.

On the afternoon of Tuesday, October 18, a convoy of cars from Bonn drove up to the house. The Justice Minister, Hans-Jochen Vogel, tried to justify to the family the government's position, explaining that the 11 hostages could well have killed again if they had been released. He could offer little sympathy; on the contrary, he prepared the family, in careful phrases, for the end.

Vogel's fears were confirmed the next day, the 19th. At about 6.00 p.m. he called Waltrude from Bonn and told her to be prepared for the worst. In a Paris newspaper, *Libération*, the Siegfried Hausner Commando had published a communiqué. It stated that the kidnappers had killed their hostage. Two hours later, he called through again with the official news of Schleyer's death. He told Jörg in stilted officialese: 'It is my unfortunate duty to tell you that the fear that I expressed to your mother at 6.25 p.m. yesterday has now been confirmed.' He then added a few personal words of regret.

Libération had meanwhile passed the text of the R.A.F. communiqué over to Bonn. It said in part: 'After 43 days we have ended Hanns Martin Schleyer's lamentable and corrupt existence. Herr Schmidt, who gambled with Schleyer's death from the beginning in his power calculations, can fetch him from a green Audi 100 with Bad Homburg registration plates from Rue Charles Péguy in Mulhouse.'

The call from *Libération* came through at 4.22 p.m. At 5.05 p.m. the Mulhouse police found the green Audi, registration HG-AN 460, in Rue Charles Péguy. Nearby streets were blocked. Judicial identification officials arrived at 5.20 p.m., but none of them dared open the car, not only because they believed that the Audi might be booby-trapped but also because there was a professional rivalry between the French Prosecutor, Jean Reynaud, and the examining magistrate in Mulhouse, Claude Meyer. Both claimed the sole right to examine and identify the corpse.

Reynaud carried the day. He demanded a bomb squad. The nearest one was on holiday. French soldiers stationed nearby offered their help, but they were refused, as were officials of West Germany's Criminal Office and the Federal Prosecutor's Office who offered to fly in German experts.

Two hours went by. Eventually at 8.00 p.m. the six nearby houses were cleared. An officer of the Sécurité Civile broke a window, and opened the bonnet and the four doors. He looked through the glove compartment and found 200 French francs. At 8.40 p.m. the boot was opened and Hanns Martin Schleyer's body was found. His face looked distorted. His grey hair was cut short. He was wearing a black-and-white striped shirt and grey-and-white trousers. He was taken into a nearby hospital.

An autopsy was undertaken by Professor Chaumont of the Institute for Forensic Medicine in Strasbourg and Dr. Priot, a local expert in forensic medicine. Schleyer had been killed by three bullets in the head. They estimated that death had occurred between 24 and 36 hours previously, i.e. between midday and midnight on October 18. In Schleyer's mouth the doctors found bits of grass. There were pine-needles on his clothing, suggesting that he had been shot in the open. He had presumably been kneeling and then fallen forward on his face.

The Audi may have been put in the Rue Charles Péguy for a reason. Péguy was a poet and philosopher who at the turn of the century turned from religion to passionate socialism. He was killed in the battle of Marne in 1914 – significantly perhaps on September 5.

Rumours concerning Schleyer's death came and went. One was that he had been strangled (it arose because one of the shots had torn across his neck). Another concerned a video-tape received by *Libération*, which sparked the rumour that his death had been filmed (in fact the only things on the video-tape were four still pictures of plastic letters announcing that Schleyer had been killed during the course of the hijacking).

Little was left to Schleyer's family now but grief and silent protest. As the burial and memorial service at Stuttgart's Stiftskirche were being prepared, the family announced that they did not want the presence of any member of the crisis staff. The crisis staff concurred. Even Helmut Kohl, the C.D.U. Chairman and a close personal friend of Schleyer, was excluded.

The only official present at the ceremony on October 25 was President Scheel. He asked in the name of the German people for the forgiveness of Schleyer's family. But that on its own would scarcely have been adequate. The events of the last few weeks had been some of the most momentous in West Germany since the end of the war. Even the building of the Berlin Wall had not touched the lives of so many West Germans so deeply. Scheel reminded those present that, however bitter they felt, Schleyer's death had not been lost for arbitrary reasons. All involved bore responsibility. Democracy, he implied, had worked, so far.

But the issue was wider even than that. The war against terrorism, he warned, would continue, internationally. All countries were potential victims. 'These young, misguided people threaten not only democratic freedoms, they are the enemies of all civilization. . . . If this flame is not extinguished immediately it will set the world alight.'

Beyond this again, looms a greater dilemma yet: is it possible for countries to react against terrorism without threatening the very freedom they seek to defend?

Governments everywhere must hope that they will not be forced to find out.

Carlos: Terror International

Dennis Eisenberg and Eli Landau

'The Japanese were bending over their suitcases. Then suddenly they straightened up. They were holding Kalachnikov carbines and hand grenades.

The whole place went crazy. As the first shots ripped through the closed hall and the first grenades exploded, nobody quite realized what was happening. The noise was appalling. People started to scream. More hand grenades exploded and hurled bodies against walls, over chairs. The noise echoed and reverberated. The chaos was total. There were more screams and people were falling, kicking legs, waving arms. The Japanese worked with horrifying efficiency . . .'

This was the massacre at Lod Airport, 1972. Just one of the horrifying triumphs of TERROR INTERNATIONAL . . .

0 552 10289 X 75p

A Coffin Full of Dreams

Frisco Hitt

THE BLOOD-SOAKED NOVEL OF A BAND OF BRUTAL CONGO MERCENARIES

At first the prisoners were silent, but not for long. They were bound to hooks, posts, and other parts of one of their trucks. Every now and then one of our blacks would get up and laboriously inflict some injury on a prisoner. A hand was cut off, a nose, an ear . . . This typified Africa for me: cutting off parts of the body. Stomachs were opened, buttocks slit, thigh-bones laid bare . . .

CORGI 0 552 10246 6 85p

CORGI

STATE OF BLOOD

THE INSIDE STORY OF IDI AMIN'S REIGN OF FEAR

By HENRY KYEMBA, former minister in the Amin government (1972-1977); Vice-President, the World Health Organization; and Chairman of the African Health Ministers.

Within months of seizing power from Milton Obote in January 1971, Amin had personally organized the massacre of thousands of his political opponents. Since that time, his rule of death has spread. His own personal corps, the State Research Bureau, kill as they wish, without fear of reprisal. They have seized judges and cabinet ministers in full public view – even from formal gatherings – taking them to what horrified onlookers knew to be certain execution. To date Amin's thugs have killed uncounted tens of thousands – some estimates say well over 100,000 a year.

Now, for the first time, a major inside figure from Uganda portrays in detail Amin's reign of terror. The result is almost unbelievable but, unhappily, true.

0 552 10558 9 FULLY ILLUSTRATED 95p